FOR, IN YOUR TONGUE, I CANNOT FIT

SHILPA GUPTA was born and lives in Bombay where she studied at the Sir J. J. School of Fine Art (1992–1997). Through her research-based practice incorporating text, drawing, objects, sound and video, she has engaged with art in its participatory, interactive and public dimensions. She has had solo shows at the Barbican in London, Contemporary Arts Center in Cincinnati and Lalit Kala Akademi in New Delhi, amongst several other venues. Her work has been shown at biennales in Venice, Kochi, Berlin and at the Museum of Modern Art, Guggenheim Museum, Tate Modern and Centre Pompidou, amongst others. In 2021, the Museum of Contemporary Art in Antwerp hosted her survey show.

SALIL TRIPATHI is a writer based in New York. A member of PEN International's board, he was chair of its Writers in Prison Committee from 2015 to 2021, and earlier co-chaired English PEN's Writers at Risk Committee. His books include *Offence: The Hindu Case*, *The Colonel Who Would Not Repent: The Bangladesh War and its Unquiet Legacy* and *Detours: Songs of the Open Road*. He is writing a book about Gujaratis. He is an award-winning journalist who has worked out of India, Singapore and Hong Kong. Salil studied at the New Era School and Sydenham College in Bombay, and at the Tuck School of Business at Dartmouth College in the US.

FOR, IN YOUR TONGUE, I CANNOT FIT

ENCOUNTERS WITH PRISON

EDITED BY
SHILPA GUPTA
AND SALIL TRIPATHI

ctxt

First published in hardback by Context, an imprint of Westland Books, a division of Nasadiya Technologies Private Limited, in 2022

Published in paperback by Context, an imprint of Westland Books, a division of Nasadiya Technologies Private Limited, in 2023

No. 269/2B, First Floor, 'Irai Arul', Vimalraj Street, Nethaji Nagar, Allappakkam Main Road, Maduravoyal, Chennai 600095

ISBN: 9789357763165

10 9 8 7 6 5 4 3 2 1

This book was published in conjunction with the exhibition
Shilpa Gupta: For, In Your Tongue, I Cannot Fit
Dallas Contemporary | 26 September 2021–13 March 2022

This project is supported in part by an award from the National Endowment for the Arts

Typeset in Le Monde Journal Std by Jojy Philip, New Delhi - 110015
Printed at Parksons Graphics Pvt Ltd, Mumbai

Including 'Untitled', 2016–ongoing,
drawings from the series on forced disappearances
by Shilpa Gupta

Table of Contents

Introduction

That the pen is mightier than sword is a phrase easy to mock. As examples from history show, distressingly, swords have killed poets for centuries. It is impossible to list all the poets who have been persecuted, for in many instances we remember their words, not their names.

And that is the point – those who wield the sword are reviled, if not forgotten; those who they slay are remembered through their words. Empires have risen and fallen and national boundaries have changed. But the words of poets have survived, passed from generation to generation through word of mouth, books and, increasingly, the internet.

In 2015, writers and filmmakers in India started returning their National Awards in protest of the growing intolerance and silencing of dissent in the country. A man had been lynched to death on suspicion of consuming beef. Writers, thinkers and activists were being murdered. First was Narendra Dabholkar. Then, writer Govind Pansare and his wife, Uma, were shot at by unidentified gunmen in broad daylight. Govind Pansare died of the bullets, while his wife survived. Next was the writer and rationalist Professor M.M. Kalburgi. An environment which we often take for granted, where one can express oneself freely, was fast slipping away. It was first sensed by fellow artists, filmmakers, writers and other activists, for whom freedom of expression is their raison d'être. A warning was being sent out to intimidate those who would express themselves differently and against majoritarianism.

In 2017, Salil evoked the power of poetry at a celebration of *Abhidhanantar*, a Marathi literary magazine, in Mumbai. In another corner of the city, Shilpa was in her studio, developing her work on the persistence of writers in the face of censorship and persecution. The two were introduced to each other by Shireen Gandhy and so the seeds to the sound art installation 'For, In Your Tongue, I Cannot Fit', dedicated to one hundred poets who have been incarcerated, were sown. Later that year, the journalist Gauri Lankesh was assassinated just outside her home in Bengaluru, and in 2018, poet and activist Varavara Rao, along with several other activists, was imprisoned. More arrests and threats have since followed, and it is now the turn of stand-up comedians, whose shows are being cancelled. Calls of 'sedition,' a word which was unheard of for several decades, have become rather commonplace.

The installation 'For, In Your Tongue, I Cannot Fit' was first shown in 2018 at the Edinburgh Art Festival and Yarat Contemporary Art Space. Since then, it has traveled to Kochi and Venice Biennale, Museum of Contemporary Art in Antwerp, the Barbican in London and most recently to Dallas Contemporary, which has helped raise a grant for this book.

In this volume, you will read many of the poems that are a part of the sound installation. The earliest poem is from the eighth century, and there are contemporary poems by poets who are still in prison, or in hiding. A few poems are in full, and some are fragments. A few are sourced from the original works, and the translations for a few are freshly commissioned for this volume. You will encounter poets as poets, poets as thinkers, thinkers as poets, students as poets, poets as professors, poets as translators, poets as publishers, poets as activists and even poets who have embraced politics. There are poets who have used poetry very directly, sometimes in mass gatherings, and those who have used poetry as oblique criticism which becomes so popular and so seeps into public consciousness that the words, and their act, have led to their arrest. There are poets who haven't been informed of the reason for their arrest, detained for several years without trials. There are poets who have had to continue living under surveillance even after being released. Sometimes it is the poet's publisher who goes to trial. Some poets have not been allowed to write poetry when imprisoned, and they have had to resort to hiding broken pencil tips in wall crevices, have had to scratch poems on soaps, or remember the lines by heart, to then write them on paper upon their release. There are poets whose writings have been banned and then smuggled out. Amongst stories of deep pain are also those where the public attention a poet-under-arrest has garnered, has generated freedom from future incarceration. One wonders: when history is scattered with examples of poets who have been flayed alive, why don't we listen more carefully to those alive today?

Alongside the poems from the installation, the editors have reached out to writers who have been in jail, writers who have experienced incarceration or persecution of other kinds, writers who have championed writers facing persecution and those who have defended poets, and compiled their original writing. Jennifer Clement writes how the act of writing itself is revolutionary; Burhan Sonmez reflects on meeting a writer in prison; Gautam Bhatia sets out the limits that the law places; Karthika Naïr's poem provides the toolkit authoritarian leaders use to curb speech; Varavara Rao's poem reminds us why his writing makes the establishment uncomfortable; Nilanjana Roy recounts the songs of the revolution; Devangana Kalita and Natasha Narwal, held in custody for a prolonged period, are inspired by the spirit of those they have encountered in jail; Umar Khalid finds solace through poetry; Dareen Tatour is deprived of a pen in the jail, because it is what her jailors fear the most; Muhammad al-Faqih Saleh writes of the raw agony of Libya; Stella Nyanzi expresses outrage over the treatment of those in jail; Yasser Khanjer yearns for freedom; Ma Thida reflects on what being in solitary confinement means; Saw Wai sees unrelenting gloom in his country; Andrei Khadanovich gives voice to Belarus's agony; André Naffis-Sahely unpacks the meaning of exile; Fatemeh Ekhtesari demonstrates what it means living away from home; James Byrne salutes the spirit of Rohingya writers in refugee camps; Ali Cobby Eckermann reminds us that prisons are not only physical; Marilyn Hacker celebrates brave voices; Malay Roychoudhury shows the meaning of iconoclasm; and Sara Hossain tells us what keeps her going in her tireless defence of writers.

You will find photographs of poems in multiple languages in this book, to represent the experience of the sound installation, where the viewers enter a sea of a hundred poems in different scripts. It is intentional that some scripts can be read and others not. Interweaving different languages to celebrate multiple ways of seeing has been integral to Shilpa's art practice, and the sound installation included poetry which could be heard and read in eight different languages – English, Arabic, Azeri, Turkish, Russian, Chinese, Hindi, Urdu and Spanish.

Shilpa has interwoven the text with her drawings, and Salil, who has written the lead essay, has filled the silences by recalling the poets' words, which, eventually, will outlive and outshine those swords. They always do.

Acknowledgements

We would like to thank all the contributors for the speed with which they agreed to participate, and the generosity of their writing. We also wish to thank Valzhnya Mort, Ma Thida, Khaled Mattawa, Lauren Pyott, Venugopal and Marilyn Hacker for translating the commissioned pieces and poems, and Gopika Jadeja, Jack Cox, Ian Probstein and Yusuf Eradam for translating other poems from the installation. Shaping the sound installation this book forms an accompaniment to has been a mammoth task while working out of a modest budget, and it would not have been possible without the support of countless researchers, volunteers, translators, interpreters, art curators, gallery assistants, friends, friends of friends and families of the poets.

We would like to thank Sara Whyatt, a human rights campaigner for twenty years, for her work in shaping the poet's introductions on the basis of Shilpa's research and her own experience. Shilpa's own research was supported by a wonderful and enthusiastic group of people spread in different parts of the world. Special thanks to Tina Marie Monelyon, who came to India from Germany, via China, and became a part of Shilpa's studio – for her many runs to sound editing studios, for her excellent handling of intricate excel sheets and for maintaining a thoughtful overview of a very complex project. Thanks to Shilpa's studio team, which swivels by the hour, from art experiments to research, from sound edits to archiving, from proofreading to countless follow-ups across different geographies and time zones – Czetan Patil for his multitasking, his precision and calm, Pooja for her sharp diligence, Prathamesh Sawant for his infectious enthusiasm, Siddhant Pitale for his rigour and attention to detail, Pranav Gogwekar for his promptness and Rahul More for his constant support. We would like to thank Yamini Shah, Anna Fech, Rizvan Alasgar, Sayara Huseynli, Ulviya Akhundova, Aynur Zarrintac, Matthew Fellion, Canan Marasligil, Cathal Sheerin, Giulia Mancini, Leonardo Sarria, Sachie Hernandez, Diana Mac-Crohon and Julie Bécourt for their research support, their enthusiasm and participation in the project.

The wonderful galaxy of supporters includes Sunil Shanbag, Ankur Tewari, Salima Hashmi, Sadagat Isayeva, Sanan Baghirov, Chloe Elder, Avaan Patel, Margherita Tinagli, Anand Thakore, Federica Beltrame, Ashish Rajadhyaksha, Sanjna Kapoor, Roshini Vadehra, Shireen Gandhy, Nidhi Goel, Rohit Goel, Melih Fereli, Omar Berrada, Tatiana Kochubinska, Moris Farhi, Wen Cuiyan, Nitika Gupta, Lia He, Quddus Mirza, Murtaza Vali, P.M. Satheesh, Ritika Bhutani, Ranjit Hoskote, Shalila Roychoudhury, Tej R. Kansakar, Hanna Vasyk, Sami Dalwai, Hidayat Marwat, Asif Sheikh, Dr David Hargreaves, Alessandro Pavone, Sherry Roush, Gavin O'Toole, Marcia Lynx Qualey, Rémi Lavalle, Nickie Shobeiry, Luca Bagnoli, Emlyn Wang, Bill Herbert, Yoav Bar, Shikha Sethi, Emily Prince, Rebecca Oliva, Dr Suzanne Fairless-Aitken, Dr Heather Kiernan and Elæ Moss. Grateful thanks, too, to Cat Lucas from Writers at Risk Programme, English PEN, and Zoë Rodriguez, chair of PEN International's Women Writers' Committee, and member of PEN International's Lawyers' Circle for her support and advice.

Finally, thank you to the poets for their generosity in allowing their works to be included in this book: from Abdellatif Laâbi, Wole Soyinka and Malay Roychoudhury to Liao Yiwu, Adonis, Dareen Tatour, Fatemeh Ekhtesari, Mehdi Mousavi, who are forced to live away from their homes, Ashraf Fayadh who is still in prison, Maung Saung Kha, who, when he last wrote, was on the move in the jungles, and Saw Wai, who has been in touch with us via someone else from an undisclosed location. Thank you to the poets and their rights-holders for giving us the permission to use their works in the installation and in this publication.

We would also like to thank Emily Edwards from Dallas Contemporary, who helped raise the support for this book. Without the encouragement of Rajiv Saini, Björn Geldhof, Maurizio Rigillo, Jane Connarty, Sorcha Carey and Valentina Costa, this complicated project would not have been possible.

For the many tyrants who don't let us sleep, there is a galaxy of supporters to allow us to dream and go on.

When I was a new officer aged 22-23,
I would conquer the world several
times a day with a red pen on the map.
My Napoleonic illness only lasted
a couple of years.

After I was discharged from the military
by a court decision and spent three
months and ten days in prison, the day
I became unemployed and broke, I chose not
to become rich, but to become a writer.
- Aziz Nesin -

Interview with Shilpa Gupta

Tina Marie Monelyon

Q: Your project, 'For, In Your Tongue, I Cannot Fit' is an experiential sound-art installation that comprises of one hundred voices which have been incarcerated from the past and the present. What brought you to this project?

A: About fifteen years ago, when I was just beginning to gain some ground in the art world, I found myself dodging all sorts of classifications, ranging from 'new media artist' to 'woman artist' and even 'young artist', which I was, once, at that time. This set me off on a research project called 'Someone Else'. It was based on a hundred books written anonymously or under pseudonyms by writers who found escape from expectations by writing under fake names, be it for reasons of prejudice ranging from gender, political persecution to choice of language, amongst many others. When I finally showed this work in 2011, I thought I had completed it, but the many stories and surprises which it had surfaced continued to hover. For example, I had not known that some of the writers I followed, say George Orwell, or even one of my favourite writers, Munshi Premchand, had such close encounters with the law. I did not know that Premchand's books were burnt and that he was once charged with sedition – a word that one thought had gone out of usage, until we recently started hearing it again. I learnt about the ghastly and violent reactions from the extreme right against the Turkish writer Aziz Nesin and read about the French writer Voltaire's time in prison. I had started collecting instances of moments when words caused discomfort to those who sought to contain imagination by restricting the mobility of a writer. This was over a decade ago, and little did one know how quickly the situation was changing and that we were heading into a similar situation here. However, that project went on the back burner, as I had become absorbed in work towards 'Altered Inheritances' – a photo work based on a hundred narratives of individuals who changed their surname, which, in fact, I was led to by Aziz Nesin.

Q: Individual liberty challenging social or State control – or control by someone wielding power – has been a recurring theme in your work. Can you elaborate on that?

A: Yes, I have long been interested in how people, or even objects, which are manifestations of their desires, traverse through systems. I used stamps that said 'Please Dispose After Use' (*Untitled*, 1995-96) and yellow-and-black adhesive tapes that said 'There is No Border Here', subverting the official declarations. I often gather material to make sense of how we construct our world and live in it. For example, in 2001, I collected cloth stained with menstrual blood to make an installation where one could not tell what it was made of, until the source was revealed. I have collected hand-drawn maps of my country, none of which match their official representation. I have spent time in the border areas where the edges of the State and definitions of morality start to blur rather visibly. In 2016, I made drawings using pigment from marijuana which was growing in the vicinity of a border check post. Over the years, one has often seen that when systems map where we are and our locations, graph where we belong, and tabulate to categorise and classify us, to seek control over us, people respond – some masquerade, some infiltrate and some catapult!

Q: And then you came to poets – tell us how that came about.

A: The sentiment of persistence echoed through the keynote speech by Salil Tripathi at the Mumbai Poetry Festival a few years ago. I did not have the opportunity to listen to it in person, but it slipped into my inbox and stirred my insides. Salil spoke passionately about the perseverance of poetry and how it returned the potential of language to the individual. Especially in times such as ours, when truth is being challenged and our agency is being frozen via coercion. I had just about restarted my project, looking at moments when writers and journalists had been incarcerated. That took a detour and found a new beginning. I started tracing the journeys of poets across time – the earliest being Abu Nuwas from the eighth century – and geography, and the risks they embraced, knowingly and unknowingly when they uttered truths to their own selves and to power. All of this went against the rapidly changing atmosphere in India, where suddenly being a liberal was an accusation and many thinkers, writers and filmmakers were targeted. I remember the very emotional moment when a friend, the filmmaker Madhusree Dutta, returned her national film award, joining the protests by the community of filmmakers and writers in India against hate being manufactured by the State. I became interested in the stories of poets and activists who wrote poetry and the power of words and the nervousness it evoked in those in power.

Q. Tell us about the title – it is unusual. Where did it come from?

A: The sound installation 'For, In Your Tongue, I Cannot Fit' is titled after fourteenth-century Azerbaijani poet Nesimi's poem. To quote a line from it: 'Both worlds can fit within me, but in this world I cannot fit'. The work looks at how speech, which is in fact the first contact we have with the world, as a form of expression, can rest in the hands of a singular structure. Poets, like writers, like artists, are dreamers – they even speak of the nightmares of the living world. The work is about the persistence of beliefs, of dreams, which make us what we are, as individuals.

Q. This book has several of your drawings in which there are missing elements. Can you explain?

The drawings are 'tracings' from found photographs around the lives of the poets. Some are from the actual moment of arrest; some from their homes, or their city from which they were forcefully removed, or in the case of Dareen Tatour, when she was placed under 'house' arrest. In others, the focus shifts to the families and supporters who stood alongside the poets. In the drawings, bodies have been left missing – making their absence more present. These absent bodies are a continuation of 'Untitled' (2016) set of drawings on the forced exit of members of the Knesset (Israel's parliament); which in turn emerge from expunged conversations in the Indian Parliament around killings of innocents by the security forces in 'Nothing Will Go on Record' (2013-14). The works are about attempts by States to arrest critique. However, words escape, and voices reverberate even more as the bodies go missing!

Q: Is there something special about poetry?

A: Poetry seems to occupy a space in our minds which is more ruptured, indirect, closer to oneself. Of all forms of writing, poetry can be quite oblique. It is the least visible too, as rarely do newspapers give enough space to poets when compared to writers and artists; rarely are books of poetry prominently stacked in bookstores, and rarely do their spines spread more than an inch. As usual, my questions led to some answers, and those created more questions. I wondered about poets who are activists and activists who write poetry, and when were these moments when they risked themselves and all that they loved so deeply, and about the attempts made to contain sounds which travel far beyond what one can see.

Q: Freedom of expression is not a new theme for you.

A: True. Some of my earliest works look at the relationship between definitions, power and human fear. We name to hold, to claim and to tame, and what those in power do today, in order to stay in power, is to name, to blame and restrain. Power likes freedom and certainty for itself and not for others. It reminds us of our death so we can approve of its killings in silence and stay silent when it raids history and erases books. Those who speak up are ridiculed, pronounced misguided and called conspirators, and trolls and bots are unleashed to harass them and to distract and confuse others. In 2008, in the context of another project, 'While I Sleep', I had the wonderful opportunity to interview Noam Chomsky. One thing that stayed with me from our conversation was when he spoke about how survey results revealed that 'most people wanted peace'. However, we live in a landscape dominated by a few, who speak the loudest, often in shrill voices, claiming to speak for others. That is why I wanted to build a chorus of ninety-nine voices – that of the multitude – who echo the poets' voices, which is the voice from the belly of a society.

Q: So, the chorus is the voice of the masses?

A: It is the intense sensation of a possible vastness of being – a kind of vibrating multiplicity – felt upon alighting from the local train here at Churchgate Station or walking in a local market, which is invariably dense, and becoming part of an overwhelming mass of people speaking a variety of dialects and languages. Therefore, upon encountering the installation and this book, you are surrounded by multiple languages and scripts, where not knowing is part of knowing.

Police detain a protester demonstrating against the arrest of writer Varavara Rao and other activists.

A poet's work?

To name the unnamable,

to point at frauds,

to take sides,

start arguments,

shape the world,

and stop it going to sleep.

– Salman Rushdie

in The Satanic Verses,

describing the poet Baal.

The Poet's Work

Salil Tripathi

The light inside the large hall was dim. I had to adjust to the darkness as I walked in and noticed the faint outline of erect spikes, dark as silhouettes, piercing through white sheets of paper. The spikes looked like flagpoles, the sheets as white flags, but not of surrender; they indicated purity. There were words on those sheets, words that have survived the dictators who sought to erase them.

Microphones hung low from the tall ceiling, meeting you at the face-level. There were one hundred of them, scattered, like hanging heads, the bodies attached to them missing. The microphones were black. You couldn't speak into them; you could only listen. Speakers within the microphones amplified voices. They were the poets' words, typed on those sheets, which the arrogant spikes had pierced in an attempt to obliterate.

But the words got passed through generations – in songs, in poems, in whispers, even in silences when memorised.

Light was let in as if reluctantly, just enough to sense the shadows, the faint outline of figures. Visitors walked around like inmates in a cell, like prison wardens. It was the light in a prison cell: not bright enough to let you read, not dark enough to let you sleep, reminding you of the brightness deprived and darkness stolen because you were a prisoner without a name in a cell without a number.

The light, like life, was outside, beyond your reach.

Some voices spoke over other voices, in Hindi, Chinese, Azeri, Arabic, English. And there were whispers. In Eastern Europe, during the communist years, it was said that when you can't trust the written word, you believe the spoken word. Words written on tiny slips of paper and read, then the paper chewed and swallowed, so that nobody would find out you that had that sheet, nobody could ever identify the handwriting. Words passed from one ear to another. Ears that listened and remembered, ears to the ground, like in Carolyn Forché's poem after her encounter with a general in El Salvador in 1978. Whispers that reverberated in the mind.

The rest was silence.

*

Shilpa Gupta's profoundly moving installation, 'For, In Your Tongue, I Cannot Fit' takes the viewer on a multisensory journey to imagine the terror, isolation and powerlessness that imprisonment imposes on a poet, simply for thinking, reflecting, expressing and writing. And how those experiences, so difficult to describe, get transformed into words of enormous power and inspiration.

This is a saga going back at least a millennium.

The installation builds on themes that have recurred in Shilpa's work. As she has said, sometimes a poet's words cause such discomfort that those in power seek to restrict imagination.

But she knew that the story was not only about India. There was Giordano Bruno, who was burned at the stake in the sixteenth century and Imadeddin Nesimi, who was skinned alive in Aleppo a century earlier for heresy. In China, Liu Xiaobo was kept in jail, released only weeks before he died, and the government didn't even permit a funeral for him; in Israel, they jailed the Palestinian Dareen Tatour for writing a revolutionary poem. There was Osip Mandelstam, who wrote from his solitary Stalin-era cell: 'You left me my lips, and they shape my words, even in silence.' And there was Nâzim Hikmet in Turkey, writing about the prisoner Halil, who 'mastered turning the pages with cuffed hands'.

*

The first protest poem I recall vividly is *Salaam,* in Marathi, by Mangesh Padgaonkar. I was a little over thirteen when Indira Gandhi declared the Emergency in India, and at fifteen, I saw her defeated in the parliamentary elections that followed in 1977. Padgaonkar's satirical poem went:

Salaam,
To everyone, salaam
To the hand that holds
And brandishes the rod, salaam
With my left hand on my rear
For fear of the boot
A right-handed salaam
To the one who closely watches me, salaam
To the one who doesn't watch and doesn't care, salaam
To the one who'd like to buy me out, salaam
To his unseen boss, who orders him to buy me out, salaam
Salaam, dear friends, to everyone, salaam.[1]

We had become fearful, anxious to protect ourselves. Padgaonkar lampooned our cowardice. He chided us, ridiculed us. He wanted to rouse us. He reminded us that even if poetry is mere words, those words can rouse. And they can trouble those with power – in recent years, governments in Cameroon, Cuba, China, India, Iran, Kazakhstan, Myanmar, Saudi Arabia, Turkey, Uganda, Vietnam, among many others, have jailed poets. Mobs have targeted and attacked poets in other parts of the world. The prognosis remains bleak. We learn to swallow our words for fear of offending the powerful.

The saga of hounding stubborn women continues in Russia. Anna Akhmatova's son was taken away to a prison camp and her fellow poets died in Soviet camps of the 1920s and 1930s. Valeria Novodvorskaya was sent to a psychiatric camp after she criticised the Communist Party in a searing poem in 1969. And Irina Ratushinskaya challenged Russian hegemony in Ukraine:

This century grows ever darker, and the next will not come soon;
To wipe clean the names off yesterday's prison wall.

Such voices question assumptions and challenge preconceived ideas, the way things are. It isn't an easy journey. The idea remains, its standard-bearers change. And one day, the world may change.

1. Translated by Vinay Dharwadker.

Recall Salman Rushdie in *The Satanic Verses:*

> *What kind of idea are you? Are you the kind that compromises, does deals, accommodates itself to society, aims to find a niche, to survive; or are you the cussed, bloody-minded ramrod-backed type of damnfool notion that would rather break than sway with the breeze? – the kind that will almost certainly, ninety-nine times out of hundred, be smashed to bits; but the hundredth time, will change the world.*

New ideas must flourish; imagination must not get crushed. But new ideas can only arise out of an unfettered mind. New ideas help us connect strands of thoughts that might seem disparate, but which are nonetheless true. And that is the role poetry plays – as Robert Frost said, a poet has a lover's quarrel with the world. The poet criticises what she sees because she loves what is being lost. Poetry is about truth, not only about facts; facts can be manipulated to serve the powerful, the poet's truth cannot. Poetry is about freedom, it is the truth staring back. It is about what cannot be valued in money or property. When told there is no money in poetry, Robert Graves replied, there is no poetry in money either.

Honouring Frost, President John Kennedy had said: 'When power leads man towards arrogance, poetry reminds him of his limitations. When power narrows the areas of man's concern, poetry reminds him of the richness and diversity of his existence, when power corrupts, poetry cleanses, for art establishes the basic human truths which must serve as the touchstone of our judgment. The artist becomes the last champion of the individual mind and sensibility against an intrusive society and an officious state. The great artist is thus a solitary figure… if sometimes our great artists have been the most critical of our society, it is because their sensitivity and their concern for justice, which must motivate any true artist, make them aware that our nation falls short of its highest potential.'

The American poet Adrienne Rich had it right. In an address at a conference she said, 'I hope never to idealise poetry – it has suffered enough from that. Poetry is not a healing lotion, and emotional massage, a kind of linguistic aromatherapy. Neither is it a blueprint, nor an instruction manual, nor a billboard.... Walt Whitman never separated his poetry from his vision of American democracy – a vision severely tested in a civil war fought over the economics of slavery. Later he called poetic lore "a conversation overheard in the dusk, from speaker far or hid, of which we get only a few broken murmurs."'

The German philosopher Theodor Adorno had asked if lyrical poetry was even possible after an act as monstrous as the Holocaust. But Rich argued that if poetry had gone mute after every genocide, there would be no poetry left in the world.

We live in a time when the liberal imagination is under threat. There is an assault on our collective consciousness and memory. Truth is tying its shoelaces, even as lies have already spread far and wide, because lies wear imported sneakers and run fast, like an idea on twitter. This idea itself isn't as new as it seems; in 1710, before even the telegraph was invented, Jonathan Swift wrote: 'Falsehood flies, and the Truth comes limping after it.' We are still tying our shoelaces while lies circle the world.

But if we listen carefully, we will find the poets – those canaries in our mines – continuing to sing. They assert that in spite of the authoritarian forces at work, humanity survives. Milan Kundera said that the struggle of people against power is the struggle of memory against forgetting. Memory reminds us of what is being lost and it does not speak in absolutes. Only seers and saints, yogis and sadhvis, imams and mullahs, it seems, speak in terms of knowing the absolute. As Pico Iyer once wrote, Indians talk in absolutes but the place abounds with relatives.

Poets are constantly seeking to unravel nuances, ambiguities and ironies; they look back in wonder. 'Against the arrogance of power, wealth, and hierarchy, poetry proposes both humility and defiance,' the Indian poet Ashok Vajpeyi wrote recently. 'Poetry offers an unannounced *satyagraha* (insistence upon the truth, or soul-force) against simplification, generalisation, and totalisation.... Poetry is a form of dynamic resistance. Poetry vitalises, rejuvenates, strengthens and expands moral imagination and moral endurance. Poetry connects time and the timeless, history and eternity. Poetry is a republic of imagination — a site where humanity matters the most.'

Rabindranath Tagore said that even a small candle illumines the world: Poetry does that at this twilight hour.

*

Anna Akhmatova saw her friend Osip Mandelstam taken away to the Gulag from which he would not return. Mandelstam had begun as a supporter of the Communist Revolution, but revolutions tend to be cruel to their thoughtful followers. Mandelstam was no exception.

But even as he was taken away to the Gulag during the Stalinist purges, he clung to his beliefs firmly, yearning for his nation to be free. He wrote in 1935:

You took away all the oceans and all the room.
You gave me my shoe-size with bars around it.
Where did it get you? Nowhere.
You left me my lips, and they shape my words, even in silence.

As I write this, Russian human rights activists who oppose Vladimir Putin's utterly unjustified and blatantly illegal attack on Ukraine, have courageously signed a manifesto condemning the war. That takes courage. A Russian-born poet who now lives in London and writes under the pseudonym Arch Hades implored the indifference of those who look at the war on their TV screens:

People want to sit on their sofas
Staring at their screens
So that when death comes,
It won't even seem
All that different

The Ukrainian-American poet, Ilya Kaminsky too criticised the apathy in his poem, 'We Lived Happily During The War.'

And when they bombed other people's houses, we
Protested,
But not enough, we opposed them but not
Enough. I was
In my bed....

Russia jailed the Ukrainian film-maker Oleg Sentsov for four years, before releasing him in a prisoner swap. His detention prompted many to write poems about him, including Darrel Petska and Tony Mochama. When I met Sentsov in New York after his release, he had a wan smile and was a picture of dignity.

Indeed, the body can be imprisoned, not the mind. Nâzim Hikmet, the great Turkish poet who spent many years in prison, wrote a poem called *Third Class Car 510,* a reference to a train which takes shackled prisoners and their captors in a designated compartment. Hikmet writes about the prisoner Halil:

> *The prisoners and guardsmen occupy the first section*
> *The sergeant hasn't smiled once*
> *Though the mausers have been laid on the racks,*
> *The handcuffs remain locked.*
> *The two sides are in different worlds.*
> *The prisoner Halil opens a book.*
> *He has mastered turning the pages with cuffed hands.*
> *This is his fifth trip*
> *In thirteen years*
> *With books and handcuffs.*
> *With lines under his eyes*
> *And white at his temples,*
> *Halil may look a bit older*
> *But his books, handcuffs, and heart haven't aged.*
> *And now, his heart more hopeful than ever*
> *Halil sits reading his book*
> *And thinking of his handcuffs:*
> *Handcuffs, we'll bear your steel into plowshares.*
> *And he finds this idea so well put*
> *That he's sorry*
> *He doesn't know the art of writing poetry.*

After some time, Halil closes his book and breathes on his glasses to clean them. He looks at the orchards and recalls the ferry of the Bosporus, the sight of Istanbul, the lights along the bay, the Topkapi palace, the streetcars, and a yellow geranium that he had grown once in prison. He looks at life.

The poet in prison is lonely. He awaits letters. Angel Cuadra, the Cuban poet, was sentenced to a fifteen-year prison term. He wrote in 1979:

> *Your letter is the poem brought by the dawn.*

But the sunlight that poets like Cuadra seek is fleeting, as is the dawn.

> *But the letter is intercepted, by falcons, and*
> *night falls like a curtain*
> *everything goes back to being like it was*
> *in front of my cell*
> *nameless*
> *endless*
> *days*
> *go by.*

From Cuba, we turn to China. Seeing her beloved husband, the Nobel Laureate Liu Xiaobo, being taken away to jail, his wife, the poet Liu Xia, wrote:

> *Every year on July 15 of the lunar calendar*
> *The river would be covered with water lanterns*
> *But they could not call back your soul…*
> *The train heading for the concentration camp*
> *Sobbingly ran over my body*
> *But I could not hold your hand…*

Prisoners live with that reality of absences, shadows and darkness. The Iranian poet Reza Baraheni, who was imprisoned by the Shah, wrote in 1973:

> *The night is like a day on the other side of the bars*
> *On this side the day is like the night.*

But there is beauty in that night too. Yannis Ritsos, the Greek poet who was jailed by the Junta in the 1960s, wrote:

Tall eucalyptus with a broad moon.
A star trembles on the water.
The sky white, silver.
Stones, flayed all the way up.
Near the shallow water you could hear
A fish jump twice, three times.
Ecstatic, grand orphanhood – freedom.

Kim Chi Ha defied right-wing military dictators in South Korea. He missed freedom in prison; more important, he missed his mother. He wrote:

You wild geese flying up in the sky,
Do you know how I feel?
Can you tell me whether my mother is standing on the new road near our shack
Waiting for my return?
Is she weeping soundlessly, looking in the direction of Seoul, wearing her out-of-season clothes?
Wild geese, tell my mother
I will return,
I will return even if I am dead –
I will break out through the walls of this jail,
I'll leap over the fence
Even if I have to sell my soul to the devil.
I will return, mother, whatever happens, I will return.

*

I have had the privilege of chairing PEN International's Writers in Prison Committee between 2015 and 2021. We have campaigned for the freedom of many incarcerated writers, poets, journalists, editors, bloggers and publishers. Many of them have been in jail for a long time. We had success in 2015 when the Cameroonian poet Emoh Meyomesse was released. While he was in jail, the French writer Alain Mabanckou wrote a letter to him, which is illuminating because it shows that when a government jails a poet, it jails much more than an individual. Mabanckou wrote:

Well, you are not alone in this captivity, because when writers are thrown in prison, they are followed in their cells by an army of readers and the loud footsteps of their outraged colleagues. It is with this optimism in mind that I am writing this letter to you, to remind you that we will never cease to speak your name and to denounce, from every rooftop of the world, the injustice that befell you and the contempt shown by the justice system towards you.

By imprisoning a writer, they are playing with fire: how could they build walls around our imagination, when they know it has a pair of giant wings and that it sings, in every season, its hymn to freedom?

We are spreading your words to the four corners of the earth, to remind the enemies of free speech that an invisible and invincible army is on its way, using words to tear down every one of the barriers keeping mankind from progress.

When a government jails a poet, it is not merely the poet that the government has sought to silence – it has also tied its own hands. Consider the story of the Burmese writer Ma Thida. When the government cracked down on demonstrators three decades ago, she was among the first to be jailed. Her health deteriorated during her incarceration. The jailors thought they would wear her down and get her to confess after long interrogation sessions. But Thida had nerves of steel. The interrogators would be tired, and she would insist that they carry on questioning her. Exasperated, one officer told her: You are in prison but you are free; we are supposed to be free, but we feel imprisoned.

Dictators are able to wield power over poets because they get the support of marginal men and women who are willing to acquiesce and be complicit – these marginal men and women are the accomplices, some of them become, in the words of Daniel Goldhagen, 'willing executioners'.

Poets have spoken out not only against political power. Their ire has been directed at economic powers too. The poet Ken Saro-Wiwa, who was among nine Ogoni environmental and human rights activists executed in 1995 by the Nigerian military, wrote this powerful poem about what freedom is, and is not:

The True Prison

It is not the leaking roof
Nor the singing mosquitoes
In the damp, wretched cell
It is not the clank of the key
As the warden locks you in
It is not the measly rations
Unfit for beast or man
Nor yet the emptiness of day
Dipping into the blankness of night
It is not
It is not
It is not
It is the lies that have been drummed into your ears for a generation

It is the security agent running amok
Executing callous calamitous orders
In exchange for a wretched meal a day
The magistrate writing into her book
A punishment she knows is undeserved
The moral decrepitude
The mental ineptitude
The meat of dictators
Cowardice masking as obedience
Lurking in our degenerated souls
It is fear damping trousers
That we dare not wash
It is this
It is this
It is this
Dear friend, turns our free world
Into a dreary prison.

Another poet who has challenged the economic order is Ashraf Fayadh, although ostensibly the charge against him is blasphemy. Like Saro-Wiwa, he is appalled by what oil has done to society's moral fibre. He is from

Palestine and lives in Saudi Arabia – he was given the death penalty, but after sustained international campaigning, his sentence has been reduced to a life term and 800 lashes. Ashraf Fayadh wrote:

losing your soul will cost time,
much longer than what it takes to calm
your eyes that have cried tears of oil
the displaced is helpless,
like blood that no one wants to buy in the oil market!
petroleum is harmless, except for the trace of poverty it leaves behind
on that day, when the faces of those who discover another oil well go dark,
when life is blown into your heart to extract more oil off your soul
for public use...
That is... the promise of oil, a true promise.

Then there are tyrants who seek to silence poets because they write in a language that the tyrants do not like. The Kazakh poet Aron Atabek has been jailed for writing in a language of his choice:

My throat, unable to speak, will die
For the sounds of my homeland.
My ancestors' patter will vanish
Like water into sand.
I am a storyteller of immortality
In Semitic and Etruscan tongues;
I am the dust of Turkic dialects
Writing in Russian.

And then there is that ultimate taboo: religion. The Saudi writer Hamzah Kashgari wrote three poetic tweets about what he thought of his relationship with Mohammed, revered as the Prophet by devout Muslims around the world.

On your birthday, I will say that I have loved the rebel in you, that you've always been a source of inspiration to me, and that I do not like the halos of divinity around you. I shall not pray for you.

On your birthday, I find you wherever I turn. I will say that I have loved aspects of you, hated others, and could not understand many more.

On your birthday, I shall not bow to you. I shall not kiss your hand. Rather, I shall shake it as equals do, and smile at you as you smile at me. I shall speak to you as a friend, no more.

Such words, expressing opinions, have led governments, religious leaders, powerful businesses and vigilantes to turn on poets and writers. But the Soviet Empire no longer exists, Mandelstam's words do; Liu Xiaobo wasn't allowed the decency of a funeral – his ashes were lowered into the ocean, as if to obliterate his existence – but he will outlive the Communist Party of China. Liu's death prompted me to write a poem, a part of which said:

> *And they were worried that if they placed his ashes in an urn and attached it to a rocket and fired it in the sky and programmed the rocket to release the urn which would scatter the ashes in space then each particle of his ashes would become a star because he was a seed and parents would name their sons after those stars*

What is it that turns men in uniform into beasts, into judges who jail people without cause, into torturers who feel nothing when they remove people's nails to extract confessions, into commanders who destroy a nation's spirit? They act with impunity, but they face the relentless gaze of the world. The poet Caroline Forche sees what she does as the poetry of witness: 'The poetry of witness reclaims the social from the political and in so doing defends the individual against illegitimate forms of coercion.' In her famous poem *The Colonel*, she writes about an encounter with a general. He recounts horrors he has overseen and challenges her by asking, 'Something for your poetry, no?'

And she responds: 'Some of the ears on the floor caught this scrap of his voice. Some of the ears on the floor were pressed to the ground.'

Poets are those ears to the ground, the eyes that see even when blindfolded, the tongues that speak long after they have been lacerated, and the minds that can't be caged. Poetry is the umbrella in Hong Kong, the cell phone in Cairo, the man in front of the tank in Tiananmen.

Albert Camus comes to mind: 'The only way to deal with an unfree world is to become so absolutely free that your very existence is an act of rebellion.'

The backlash continues. Parul Khakhar is a Gujarati poet who wrote soothingly rhyming poetry that was never considered political. She wrote ghazals and songs, and the authorities praised her, until she was appalled by what she saw – the sight of dead bodies floating in the river Ganga, the holiest of rivers for devout Hindus, when the second wave of the pandemic overwhelmed India and countless people died. Stunned by governmental callousness, she wrote a poem, *Shab-Vahini Ganga,* comparing the river with a hearse, which I translated.

> *Flames rise high and reach the sky, the furious city rages;*
> *O King, in your Ram-Rajya, do you see bodies flow in the Ganges?*

Overnight, she became a public enemy for the very readers and patrons who had earlier claimed to like her, and she received exceptionally vile abuse. She wasn't charged under any law – expressing sympathy for the dead is not yet an offence – but she was intimidated enough to lock her social media profile. And yet, she remains undeterred; she has been writing in Gujarati magazines, with veiled, nuanced responses to those who criticise her. In a recent poem (which too I translated), she explained her silence:

> *The pain will get unbearable, but you will not speak;*
> *Even if your heart will scream, you will not speak*

We cannot let ephemeral events silence our voices. As Baal says in *The Satanic Verses,* the poet has to stop the world from going to sleep. We must stay awake. And one day, into that heaven of freedom where the mind is without fear and the head is held high, as Tagore envisioned in his *Gitanjali*, we shall awake.

Shilpa Gupta's tribute to brave poets holds a mirror in front of us, forcing us to look.

We must.

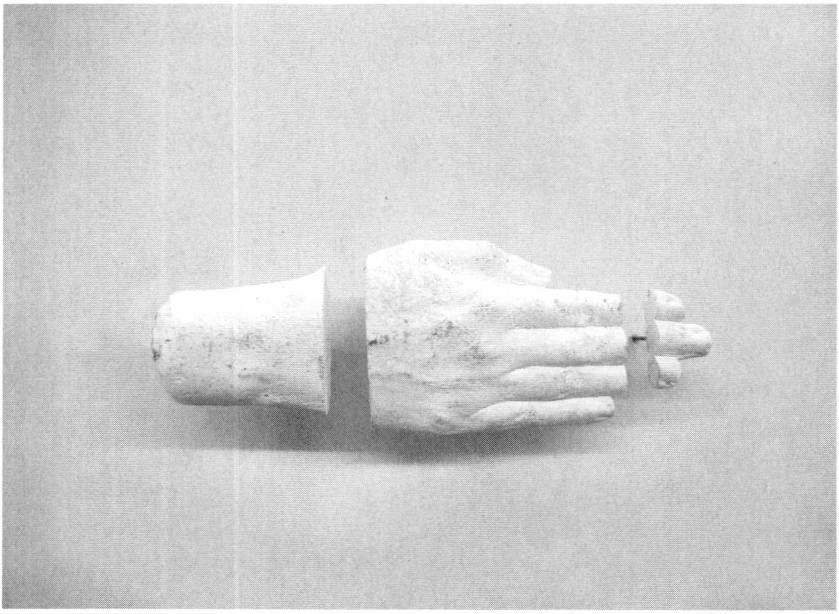

The Act of Writing a Poem Is in Itself an Act of Revolution

Jennifer Clement

When I think of the poets incarcerated in the world and punished, I think of poetry. Poetry is almost the only thing that has no monetary value. You cannot sell a poem. Nobody wants to buy a poem. Poems are not for sale in the market by the apples and peaches, or in the auction houses by sculptures and paintings. I confess that it gives me a strange wonder and shock to think that a poem is so powerful and so dangerous that a poet can be locked up and sometimes sentenced to death for rhymes and couplets, for metaphors and symbols.

When contemplating how dangerous poems have become, I recall the words of British poet and novelist Thomas Hardy: 'If Galileo had said in verse that the world moved, the Inquisition might have let him alone.' In our times, if Galileo had inked his discoveries in free verse with stanza breaks, he would likely be looking at the sky – his round, telescope-shaped sky – from a prison cell. A poet can write, as Palestinian poet Ashraf Fayadh has written among other verses: 'Earth is the hell prepared for refugees', and be sentenced to death (now reduced to eight years in prison and 800 lashes) in Saudi Arabia.

Mahvash Sabet, imprisoned in Iran in 2008 and freed ten years later in 2017, penned impassioned poems to Fariba, with whom she shared a cell at the beginning of her incarceration. Sabet wrote: 'O my companion in the cage! How many cruelties we saw together; how many favours too and blessings in our isolation. [...] They tied your wings to mine, feather to feather, and you rested your head beside mine every night.'

The poet Li Bifeng, in China, continues to compose poems in prison, where he has been since 1998. One stanza begins: 'Over the high wall, we watch the sun from afar and the mountains from afar. In the dreams of nights, we see people from afar using the net of yearning we salvage those scattered memories and then we let the bones grow into the bones.'

In 2017, I visited Dareen Tatour, the Palestinian poet who was under house arrest and awaiting sentencing. She gave me a cloth she had embroidered in red thread with the words: 'Poetry is not a crime!'

In honouring poets who live in peril, I think of how, in my fidelity to empirical knowledge, poetry is my secular faith and where I find revelation. Poetry is the search for truth and solace before the invisible. And every poet knows this: although stars may have different names in all the world's languages, they cast the same light.

The act of writing a poem is in itself an act of revolution.

Poet, Good Horseman

Burhan Sonmez

I met İlhan Sami Çomak two years ago, when I visited him in prison. Poets are special people, they are known as such, they are difficult to reach. To reach İlhan, it was necessary to pass through the thick walls and iron bars behind which he weaved his poems. I wished that he himself could pass through the walls and bars, come this way, to the streets where our lives spread. I turned from side to side through the labyrinth-like corridors of Istanbul's Silivri Prison, where approximately 30,000 prisoners were held, and finally entered a meeting room. While I waited, I wondered if the beautiful poems created in this dampness were worth all the pain. I realised that there are no scales to weigh freedom. After a while, the door opened and İlhan, whom I knew from his photographs, walked in. As the stillness of a photograph makes one feel the passing time, it gives people grief. İlhan, who stood in front of me with his blood and life, was also spreading the same sadness. He was tall, thin. He looked like a horseman. If he could get through those irons, he would have jumped on his horse and gone, no matter where.

He has been behind walls for twenty-seven years. He was a twenty-two-year-old geography student at the University of Istanbul when he was arrested in 1994. He was tortured for alleged ties to illegal Kurdish organisations and was sentenced to life imprisonment. Those years were the most violent period of the Kurdish civil war; thousands were killed and thousands imprisoned. There are many writers in prison. The number of students alone is 70,000. Both a poet and a student, İlhan is one of Turkey's longest-serving political prisoners.

İlhan didn't give up. He has published eight poetry books. While writing poetry, he also continued his demand for justice. He requested a retrial to prove his innocence. The European Court of Human Rights ruled that İlhan's prosecution was unlawful in 2007. His conviction was appealed in 2013 and 2016, but his life sentence was reconfirmed in a session where the court didn't listen to him, to his lawyers or to the witnesses at all.

İlhan is one of the leading poets of his generation. In his latest book, *I Came To You*, which won the 2019 Sennur Sezer Award, he said: 'There is no city we need to reach. Everything is here. / Open the window. Open it as the horses whinny / in the wideness of the world. Open it without speaking / of the shortness of summer, of never-ending winter.'[2]

İlhan and I studied in different departments of the same university a few years apart. We had not met at the time. When we saw each other in the meeting room of the prison, we hugged like two friends meeting in the university canteen after the summer vacation. The wheel of time turns slowly in prison, and man's movements slow down. İlhan carried that slowness with simplicity. His voice was soft. He spoke unhurriedly, using elegant words. We talked about our university years, and Istanbul, and our villages, which we realised were very far apart but very similar to each other. We mentioned the names of books and authors.

He had the right to have seven books in his ward at one time. 'That's what my books and my poems are, my life here,' he said. I told him about the interest his poems received abroad, and that events were organised in his name. Many people were reading his books and fighting for his freedom. By saying all this, I was trying to show him that he was not forgotten behind the walls, that he was not alone. I wanted him not to lose hope.

İlhan then spoke of the emptiness in his mind. His facial expression was more emphatic than the words he used. He said he could no longer envision the reality of life outside. 'I try to remember,' he said, 'I try to imagine that I was once outside, walking the streets of Istanbul, but my mind does not perceive. I lost my sense of reality about my life outside. It's like I was born here in prison and what I know about the world is either what I've heard from visitors or read in books.'

When I came out of prison on that warm autumn day, I felt that I had left my brother, who had not been able to see the world outside since he was twenty-two, rather than a poet. I carried with me his words that had been hammered into my mind like a thick nail.

2. Translated by Caroline Stockford.

Cast of open mouth in gun metal

You Can't Always Say What You Want: Free Speech and the Law

Gautam Bhatia

Poets and poetry have sometimes been caught in the crosshairs of the law. Poetry's facility in communicating multiple – and fluid – sets of meanings, its embeddedness in the cultural life of a society, and its use to challenge dominant social norms, as Lila Abu-Lughod does in *Veiled Sentiments: Honour and Poetry in a Bedouin Society*, have made the form a particularly prominent target of censorship by State and non-State actors. From Osip Mandelstam to the poetry of Mahmoud Darwish, from Nâzim Hikmet to Federico Garcia Lorca, examples are rife of poets – and poems – that have threatened both State and social power.

As far as the contemporary legal landscape is concerned, the rights of poets – and restrictions upon them – are not specific, but fall within the broader domain of the right to freedom of expression (and the limitations placed upon it). There is a line of argument that there deserves to be a specific right, within the right to freedom of expression, that applies to *artistic* expression. A stand-alone right to the freedom of artistic expression first appeared in the inter-war Weimar Constitution, and has been since incorporated (for example) into the constitutions of Germany, Austria, Switzerland, Italy, Spain, Greece, Argentina, Colombia, Peru, Chile, South Africa and the Congo.[3]

That said, however, whether or not constitutions guarantee specific rights to freedom of artistic expression, poets – and artists – have by and large been subjected to the same regimes of restrictions and censorship as other individuals, depending on whichever jurisdiction they find themselves in. Some courts have, on occasion, recognised that art might require to be judged by internal standards that are not always the same as the standards used to judge non-artistic forms of expression. We can see this approach, for instance, in the South African Constitutional Court's holding that parodies

3. Eleni Polymenopoulou, 'Freedom of Art' in *The Max Planck Encyclopedia of Comparative Constitutional Law.*

do not ordinarily violate copyright law (*Laugh It Off Productions*[4]) or the German Constitutional Court's observation that art creates its own 'aesthetic reality' (*Esra*[5]). Such observations aside, not many courts have taken the argument to its logical conclusion, of granting art more latitude.

For this reason, a consideration of the interface between poetry, the freedom of expression and the law will need to fall back upon the range of proscriptions that are generally applied to limit expression, with a specific focus on art and poetry.

In contemporary times, perhaps the most relevant and topical of these restrictions is that of hate speech. Hate speech legislation exists, ostensibly, to protect equal rights and dignity, especially of groups and communities that have been – and continue to be – subjected to discrimination, persecution and violence based on their identity. Hate speech recognises that these harms can be caused both by acts and by words, and often words are integrally constitutive of the *practise* of discrimination. Determining what constitutes hate speech, thus, is contextual enquiry, which examines speech and expression in its historical setting, and in the context of the relationship between the speaker, the audience and the target of the speech. While the determination of what constitutes hate speech may be relatively straightforward in certain respects (see, for example, the discussion around homophobic expression as hate speech in the Canadian Supreme Court case of *Saskatchewan vs Whatcott*[6] or caste slurs as hate speech, as held by the Indian Supreme Court in *Swaran Singh vs State*[7]), the enquiry becomes considerably more complex in the case of art and artistic expression because of the fluidity of meaning and because of the gap between the artist's own intention or views, and what is contained in the artwork.

Thus, even if we agree that there is a broad consensus within constitutional liberal democracies across the world (this spans jurisdictions in Europe, Latin America, Africa and countries such as Canada and India) over what,

4. *Laugh It Off Productions vs South African Breweries*, 2005 (8) BCLR 743 (CC); the case involved a parody of the respondent's brand upon a T-shirt.
5. BVerfGE 119, 1; the case involved a novel featuring characters who were identifiable in real life.
6. *Saskatchewan vs Whatcott*, [2013] 1 SCR 467; the case involved the distribution of pamphlets with homophobic messages in a school.
7. *Swaran Singh vs State of Punjab*, CA No. 1287 of 2008; the case involved the use of the caste slur 'chamaar'.

in principle, constitutes hate speech, its application to artistic expression can prove fraught and controversial. In the case of poetry, a good example is the judgment of the South African Equality Court in *Afri-forum vs Malema*, which involved the singing of an anti-Afrikaaner 'struggle song' from the apartheid era, which had the lyrics 'Shoot the farmer/shoot the Boer'. The South African Equality Act has one of the classic modern formulations of hate speech, explicitly linking it to equality and non-discrimination. In *Afri-Forum*, the song lyrics in question were held to be hate speech against Afrikaaners, notwithstanding the origins of the song in the struggle for a democratic South Africa, and its legacy as a song associated with the freedom movement. The Equality Court held that this history did not alter the fact that the lyrics, as analysed *today*, amounted to hate speech.

Needless to say, the decision generated significant controversy, and demonstrates the difficulties in applying the law of hate speech to artistic expression, even where it is done with the best of intentions, and with the right principles in mind. It is equally trite to note that such laws are *not* always applied with the best of intentions: not only hate speech laws, but also anti-terror and sedition laws have been deployed against writers and poets. A recent example is the incarceration of the Palestinian poet Dareen Tatour for 'inciting violence'.

Secondly, poetry and artistic expression have often fallen foul of blasphemy legislation. In the case of blasphemy laws, regional charters and legal instruments have proven particularly ineffective, as they have accorded a wide margin of appreciation to national legislatures to determine when to curtail speech in order to preserve the 'equal rights of others' or their 'dignity'; as seen, for example, in the jurisprudence of the European Court of Human Rights, interpreting the European Convention of Human Rights. If we look at court judgments and laws that have sought to justify restrictions upon, or control over, artistic expression on grounds of blasphemy (or religious insult), whether it is in India, Indonesia or the United Kingdom (three historically prominent offenders in this regard), we find that a common set of arguments are deployed from *within* what can be called 'the liberal tradition'. (I do not here propose to deal with jurisdictions that explicitly disavow freedom of expression as a constitutional value or make it outrightly subordinate to religious sentiment;[8] These sets of arguments

8. Gautam Bhatia, 'Religious Speech', in *The Oxford Handbook on the Freedom of Speech*.

coalesce around 'balancing' the right to freedom of expression with other, equally important constitutional values – primarily, pluralism and equal respect. In *form*, therefore, these arguments are similar to the argument for proscribing hate speech; in substance, they are considerably more dubious. On excavating a little further, one finds that their defence of pluralism and equal respect boils down to a public right *not to be offended or insulted* (and not a public right not to be *discriminated* against). In comparative freedom of speech doctrine, this is known as the 'heckler's veto', as it allows for the freedom of artistic expression to be subordinated to what are *subjective* claims of offence or indignity; furthermore, the justification flowing from the respect for pluralism is based on the premise that it is for individual communities to draw lines around what is deemed tolerable or acceptable, and to exercise absolute authority to police those lines.

Closely related to blasphemy laws – and following similar logic – are obscenity laws, where injured public morality replaces injured religious faith. The prosecution of poets for obscenity has a long lineage, with the trial of Oscar Wilde for 'gross indecency' heading the list. And as recently as 2015, the Indian Supreme Court refused to quash obscenity proceedings against a poet over his poem on Gandhi, noting that 'historically respectable personalities' could not be subjected to insult, even in art.[9]

Freedom of expression in general – but, for our purposes, freedom of artistic expression in particular – is affected not simply by the content of laws, but also the procedure that is deployed to implement them, an issue to which we now turn.

Jurisdictions across the world are divided along whether they allow prior restraint, or not. Put simply: is the State authorised to *ban* a creative work (whether a book, a play or a poem) so that it never sees the light of day? Or is it limited to proceeding against the *artist* (whether under civil or criminal law), but not authorised to take the work itself out of the marketplace of ideas? Perhaps most famously, the United States forbids 'prior restraint' almost entirely, in keeping with its minimalist approach to outright restrictions on the freedom of expression. Similarly, the American Convention on Human Rights stipulates, in express terms, that the freedom of speech 'shall not be

9. *Devidas Tuljapurkar vs State of Maharashtra*, (2015) 6 SCC 1.

subject to prior censorship but shall be subject to subsequent imposition of liability'.[10] This may be contrasted, for example, with the legal position in India, where the Code of Criminal Procedure explicitly lays down a process under which state governments may ban books or other forms of art, which will then have to be challenged in a judicial forum by the artist.[11] The distinction is a crucial one for artistic liberty: a power to *ban* makes censorship costless for the State, and leaves the material and financial burden of *exercising* artistic freedom upon creators, who must move court to have the ban overturned. A denial of such power, on the other hand, places the burden upon the State to prosecute cases where it believes that an artist has violated the law.

To sum up, the relationship between the artist or poet, freedom of expression and the law is a fraught one. Across the world, two of the most common provisions under which artists are prosecuted, or their works banned, are blasphemy laws and hate speech laws. While the latter is presumptively more legitimate than the former, in a democracy, the implementation of both has been controversial and has often been seen as judicial overreach. The freedom of artists and poets is also affected by whether the legal regime allows the State to ban artistic production, or not; on this, there is no general consensus between jurisdictions, but far too many countries continue to vest the power to ban books in the hands of executive authorities.

10. Article 13, American Convention on Human Rights.
11. Sections 95 and 96, Code of Criminal Procedure, India.

Handbook for Aspiring Autocrats

Karthika Naïr

Address your future subjects as equals on the first day – centurions, mitron, countrymen or tovarisch, tongzhi, samakmit, behenon aur bhaiyon…(whichever variant applies) – and allude to yourself as their servant, soldier. **B**irth fears, real and fictive, rapidly, with well-chosen words that bring to mind amorphous, appalling evils: apostasy, communism, deep state, devil-worship, godlessness, insurgency, islamo-gauchisme, marxism, nihilism, pederasty, external aggression…(whichever variant or variants apply): words that may mean anything or nothing, chameleon words to beget followers and soon beleaguer every free-thinker. **C**aptivate the nation with blarney on a golden past, and your credence in rare, glorious bloodlines that connect right back to divinity. **D**iscredit them all, those historians, the idiot journalists, the thoughtless scientists who differ on any of many inconvenient (cursedly undeniable) facts. **E**rode the credibility of all these adversaries with one or several of the slurs *anti-national, bourgeois, communist, liberal, neo-colonialist, traitor,* also *urban-naxal*…(whichever variant applies), embroider lore impossible to expunge with reality. **F**orge new myths – on the greatness of the mother-state, on rightful heirs to land and power, on an ancient unchanging culture; foster a cult around your own austere, prodigious self: flaunt your writerly, painterly, artistic, athletic or heroic prowess (whichever variant or variants apply…) at each occasion then flood all public platforms with accounts of your inspiring altruism, your benevolent leadership, your worship of every currently holy cow; while at it, fabricate tales of valour as well: ones featuring crocodiles, bare chests, or bears, for instance. [**G**lorify womankind, do not forget, but solely as wives and mothers, group these creatures as extensions of breasts and wombs and other bobs of flesh, to be garlanded and guarded though never granted autonomy over their selves. **H**arness the women whose voices and pens haze your aura by haranguing them in tones of gentle, pained reproof with the terms elite, men-haters, pawns of foreign states, presstitutes, trollops, unfeminine… (whichever variant or variants apply).] **I**mpress your portrait and patronym – ideally with sobriquets like Bhavishya ki Aasha or First Brother or Il Duce – on every surface: airport hoardings, hotel lobbies, comics and fairy tales, medication, ID cards, textbooks, vaccine certificates and stadia, for the populace to idolise you as saviour, as metonym for all progress. **J**ail books and songs and plays that jeopardise your vision of the world, of the past and present, or your own austere, prodigious self; yes, jag with iron spikes those books and songs, broadsheets and plays that jinx your well-laid plans for this new nation or jolt their way into the heads and hearts of your people with whispers from truth; jell their mouths with ice or adhesives so no unfriendly words nor sounds jackknife their way into ears through airwaves. **K**indle prejudice and resentment among the vast, privileged majority with reports of persecution and injustice and insult, keep them perennially on edge till they kill at ease for imagined slights and hazards. **L**asso language, but quietly, lace its feed with opiates and lance its tongue so it lilts no more anthems of resistance; laud poets, playwrights, essayists and novelists as "engineers of the human soul", then lynch them at ceremonial events through praise leavened with not-so-hidden censure. **M**arshall spies by the sidelines to monitor domicile, expression, genealogy, also verse, line and stanza: everything is future munition to manacle their words. **N**eutralise them, the poets, the novelists, the essayists and editors, by naming spouses, lovers, offspring (whichever variant or variants apply…) in offences rumoured and invented: nail the bastards through their kin, yes, nail them.

Outlaw all those words, words by Allende and Llorca and Zweig, Benyamin and
Mandela and Ying-Tai and so many more, words that overhang sleep, night after
night: obscure their light, outrun their resonant heartbeat; to that end, oppress press
and publishers with
menace or money or both;
occupy the judiciary and own
every organ of law and order. **P**ersecute
them poets, playwrights, editors and novelists,
also peace- keepers and sceptics, philosophers and
rationalists should they protest your policies; punish the
comedians, the satirists – and if they have not yet parodied
you in public, or piqued your preferred minions, pull them in for
thought crime, place them under lock and key for evil intent, for pillorying
the sacred values of nation, civilisation, caste, creed, blood… (whichever variant
or variants apply). **Q**ualify your illustrious predecessors (especially the dead) as
libertine, poltroon, opportunist, or stooge of the Empire (whichever
variant or variants apply); quaff any flagrant triumphs as your own;
quarry their symbols, their stories, their successes out
of collective memory to quench the disquiet in your
breast. **R**emove the poet's spectacles, retrieve
the writer's safety pins, restrain their
access to paper so they can
neither read nor write
(nor relay thoughts
through soap or cigarette rolls or walls), cannot raise the words, the thought, that
could rouse thousands to reflect, to react, in turn. **S**et fire to the Kamasutra, slash the
Song of Solomon – sentence desire as alien scourge – and spur your lackeys to strike
out Bama and Sukirtharani from syllabi of future teachers, historians,
scholars, writers – from the eyes of adults, if feasible. **T**hreaten
the children of poets and other agitators, tear them
away from their parents' gaze and embrace,
throw them in prison but try to keep them alive (the
dead tack low in trade- offs). **U**surp land and livelihood and
nationality, freedom too if you can, from peasants and aborigines,
labourers and believers of other faiths, all those you uglified for your own gains, then
unleash armies of thugs and rioters on them. **V**accinate your people with
vicious, vain beliefs during a pandemic – vandalise the cures and
programmes of all but your allies; value perceived
victory over the lives of thousands, or tens of thousands. **W**age
war, real or fictive, on neighbouring or weaker states; warble the names of
holy grails and invented perils as reason; wall up the opposition, reasonable generals
(if any remain) and wise statesmen (if any remain), for fair warnings to
the forces or to citizenry. **X**erox your hates, your greed, and above
all, your xenophobia, on to corporate associates; xeriscape the nation
into murderous rivers and famished plains, into burgeoning mines and
ravaged wildlands. **Y**aw Time, and yank it back, long back, lest you yellow
with Age and yield to Death, two forces few can yoke to stillness. **Z**oomorphize
as the nation's sacred beast; zhng your own austere, prodigious self into immortality.

Poetry[12]

Varavara Rao

Translated from Telugu by N. Venugopal

Poetry
Truth that need not be concealed
People who do not need a government
Life that doesn't need ambrosia

If you search my pockets
Ransack the books and papers on my table
And the racks on the shelves
Pry open my flower-like ribcage
There is no secret other than poetry

My dangerous personality
That you do not understand
The secret is poetry

Look carefully
It is like moonlight trapped in a rectangle
In an arrogant pose
You look up to insult me
See, my poetry shines in the blue sky as a full moon
You see the moon and are shocked
But surprisingly the moon cannot see himself in this cell

I used to feel disgusted
When you were combing my body

12. Written in jail on 30 December 1987, when the poet was an undertrial prisoner in the Secunderabad Conspiracy Case (1974–1988) and the Ramnagar Conspiracy Case (1974–1988). He was later acquitted as 'not guilty' in both the cases.

Now
After I poured out all my blood
And transfused it with poetry
To be my company in solitude
I pity you thinking your search in my lap
Is for your lost child of humanity
When you grope around my neck
Your metal detector trembles on my chest
I surrender myself to you
As if I am exploring my own secret worlds
Uncovering me and peeling my own skin
To hear my own poetic voice
And to feel the appeal of touch

In your hands that shackle me
Poetry descends like a heavy weight
As you attach a chain

Whenever I move
Noise of soaring free birds

In the daylight of court
Prosecution's conspiracies come out

You go on shadowing
Poetry gets ignited and continues to fire
You go on ruling
Poetry talks about people even in sleep
You throw the net of death and keep waiting
Poetry swims in consciousness just before your eyes

Poetry is an open secret that annuls the state
Even as it is taking shape in my heart
It reaches those it must
It is understood unconsciously
Even as it is rising in my imagination

It inspires movements
The secret is that
My poetry took birth with the movement's first milk

My poetry
Continues to flow like a blood letter stream
Out of your hands that closed mine
Like a broken string of pain and thread of anger
Like the sight that lights tears

One Song at a Time

Nilanjana Roy

What you remember, two years after that freezing winter in Delhi, is the broken glass and the lathi-charges, the gunmen on the streets threatening women protestors and unarmed students, the teargas, the blood spilled on pavements and zebra crossings, the young people of your city herded into buses, or jailed under draconian laws, some still awaiting trial and an elusive freedom; you remember the boots of policemen, the grim bars of their prison vans, the water-cannons, the smoke rising into the night.

And you remember tiny earthen cups of chai, warming everyone's hands in those two–degree centigrade nights, and you remember the songs that streamed forth, unstoppable, those songs of freedom.

*

In December 2019, protests erupted all across India as Narendra Modi's government passed the divisive Citizenship Amendment Bill. The CAA, coupled with the National Register of Citizens, uses religion as the yardstick to determine whether undocumented migrants from countries neighbouring India can be fast-tracked for Indian citizenship if they apply for it, provided they are from several specific religions, not including Islam. This goes against the spirit of the UN Refugee Convention, which grants asylum rights to anyone, regardless of faith, if they have well-founded grounds to fear persecution. India hasn't signed the Convention, but until recently, abided by the norms.

The papers and documentation required by the proposed Register also constitute a tricky citizenship test. Ostensibly implying that there is no clarity about whether those already living in India are citizens or not, the Register means to certify their status. In effect, Indians can be called upon to produce documents that prove they or their ancestors have lived in the country since 1971, the year in which Bangladesh was founded, making a distinction between those who moved to India in that tumult and 'Bangladeshis', who are perceived to have settled in the country without due process in later decades. This is a fraught demand that places the burden of proof of being an Indian on the individual rather than on the State to prove otherwise. Bitter debates have broken out, with many arguing that these new legal instruments would change the plural nature of the country, and across India, Muslims have expressed fears that they could in effect lose citizenship if these acts, taken in concert, became law.

In any conflict between a government and its people, a State and its citizens, the State holds the power. An authoritarian government can control and muzzle the media, can render democratic and parliamentary checks and balances completely ineffective, can threaten the independence of the judiciary. It can also unleash terrifying laws such as India's UAPA, the Unlawful Activities (Prevention) Act, once used against institutions and groups of individuals suspected of engaging in terrorism and broadened in 2019 to apply to individuals. Its draconian provisions allow the State to arrest individuals on suspicion, hold them in judicial custody for a longer period, and make it virtually impossible for an accused to get bail until trials (often delayed for years) are completed. Authoritarian regimes can and do use the police and paramilitary forces as a powerful tool to crush protests.

What is left to people, then? 'If Parliament is yours, the streets are ours', one defiant poster in Delhi said. This is what happened, incredibly: in the middle of a particularly cold December, a group of Muslim women sat down on the highway near Shaheen Bagh in New Delhi. They said their sit-in would continue until the black laws were repealed. The State had muscle and gunmen on its side. The women of Shaheen Bagh had only solidarity, and the power of their voices, rising in a collective chant to demand and celebrate 'azadi', freedom.

*

You collect stories from around India, as the protests spill from Assam in the north-east to Aligarh in Uttar Pradesh in the north, as the spirit and resolution of Shaheen Bagh, where the Indian flag is mounted on the barricades alongside posters of Mahatma Gandhi, B.R. Ambedkar and other leaders of the freedom movement, spills over to Dimapur in Nagaland, Kolkata in West Bengal, to Hyderabad and Bengaluru in the south, and other cities across India, from Kanpur, Kishanganj, Chennai to Chandigarh.

On 13 December, there is a tense confrontation between the crowds of students and protestors massed at the gates of Assam's Dibrugarh University. Violent protests against the NRC have started to rock the state, vehicles have been set on fire; the Central Reserve Police Force has been called out. As the CRPF men approach, armed and with permission to fire at the crowd, something incredible happens. 'I remember, we told each other, "sing, sing,"' student David Hazarika tells journalists later. 'If we sing, they can't do anything.'

The crowds break into the national anthem; by tradition, you rise to your feet as a mark of respect when Rabindranath Tagore's *Jana Gana Mana* is sung, and stay at attention, hands by your side. The CRPF men lower their revolvers, confused. This happens thrice; the crowd versus the men in uniform, raising their voices to sing Tagore's words again and again, pitting a song against guns and teargas. Incredibly, it works.

*

The temperature drops in Delhi. At Shaheen Bagh, and other protest sites, volunteers bring in blankets and offer rounds and rounds of chai. If you sit with the women through one of those long nights, you forget the bitter chill in the glow of conversation, your heart lifts with a sudden, unexpected love for the Constitution as first a hundred, and then a thousand, and by January 2020 tens of thousands of voices recite the Preamble to the Indian Constitution in unison:

'WE, THE PEOPLE OF INDIA, having solemnly resolved to constitute India into a SOVEREIGN SOCIALIST SECULAR DEMOCRATIC REPUBLIC and to secure to all its citizens' – those magical words, justice, liberty, equality and fraternity, spoken in the constituent assembly on 26 November 1949 – 'do HEREBY ADOPT, ENACT AND GIVE TO OURSELVES THIS CONSTITUTION…'

Protests are not just movements raised in opposition to a divisive idea, an autocratic government – they can become a movement that binds people together, as they discuss, night after night, what a country should be, how we should express fraternity towards one another. If governments have the crushing weight of brute force, the people have the promises of the Constitution, and they have poetry to hold up as a shield and a comfort against the dark, blood-streaked moments when the Jamia Millia University library is teargassed, or students are shot at by their own police, when the roads and chowks turn into battlefields.

On 21 December, the poet, lyricist and performer Varun Grover steps up to the mike and takes the informal stage made of rickety tables. He recites a new poem, borrowing a little of the music from the Bangladeshi Baul musician Shah Abdul Karim, a little of the spirit of his words from the shayari of Rahat Indori.

'*Hum kagaz nahi dikhayenge*,' he begins, and the crowd quietens, sensing that something true is in the air. 'We will not show our papers.'

It becomes an anthem, chanted by dissenters across all of India: 'Dictators will come and go, the NRC papers we will not show, you blind us with teargas, you poison our waters, that our love will sweeten, and we'll drink it all in one go.'

*

One evening, in the narrow, crowded alleys of Daryaganj, outsiders torch a car, trying to fan trouble between the police and the massive numbers of protestors gathered at an anti-CAA rally. The air in Delhi is electric with danger, loud with slogans; you sense a desperation in the ranks of the ruling party's supporters, a fear that these protests will ignite like flying embers across the nation, feeding the growing discontent with the regime.

By now, outsiders have tried unsuccessfully to provoke students into less peaceful ways of protesting, and later on, gunmen will appear in front of universities, opening fire at students and at the massed ranks of women. In Lucknow, women protesters are threatened with cases, their blankets and water bottles snatched away by local police, called anti-national because they sing about azadi – an old feminist protest song, constantly repurposed, its lyrics shifting with each generation – demanding 'nafrat-hinsa se azadi', freedom from hate and attacks such as the lynchings of Muslims that have become a dreadful feature of post-2014 India.

You hear from a friend, a brilliant photographer, that he ran for his life with others, trying to use his press card and his body to shield young boys from the blows of lathis. Those alleys, the next day, have sprouted torn chappals and shoes, powdered glass shattered so fine that it gleams like snow, though it leaves lacerations on your ankles. Your friend says that the police caught a few boys and beat them mercilessly, saying, 'Here, here is your freedom.' And that two of the boys escaped, and as they ran, they sang to the police, '*Sun lo Modi, hum leke rahenge azadi*' (Listen, Modi, we won't rest until we've reclaimed our freedom).

*

The strange power of songs is that they can capture all that is censored or that people are afraid to speak out aloud. Poets record what could be left unrecorded in authoritarian times; they sing of the dark times, yes, but they also stand in the way of the perpetual amnesia that marks our endlessly scrolling era. Aamir Aziz, famous for his searing blues, refuses to allow the wave of lynchings to be forgotten, in his *Ballad of Pehlu Khan*.

'On my Aadhar card, my name is Aamir Aziz, and this is enough to get me into trouble. These songs, this poetry, it is a compulsion. How else can an artist respond to the horror and pain?' he says in a 2020 interview.

In March 2019, before the CAA–NRC protests, he wrote *Acche Din Blues* – the Blues for the 'good days' – a reference to the first and most popular slogan of Modi's government: 'achchhe din aane wale hain', or, happy days are coming soon:

> *You write 'injustice' on the earth;*
> *We will write 'revolution' in the sky.*
> *Everything will be remembered;*
> *Everything recorded.*

In the aftermath of the protests, your city will see terrible riots and injustice, will see a long, dark time when the innocent are jailed and others hounded.

Those who lit the fires of violence are set free and rewarded by their political mentors. But every so often, even through the COVID pandemic, a wall will speak, the graffiti reminding you: '*Sab yaad rakha jayega* – everything will be remembered.'

And in Assam, where the Miyas – descendants of Muslim migrants from elsewhere in India who have lived for generations on the shifting char chapori, the sandbanks and river islands – are now threatened and persecuted by the citizenship laws, their poems eloquently speak of the fear of being named a 'D-Voter' ('Doubtful Voter') or of being sent to detention centres. In 2016, Hafiz Ahmed, a writer and president of the Char Chapori Sahitya Parishad, a body that promotes Assamese language and literature among the people who live on the char chapori, wrote:

Write
Write Down
I am a Miya
My serial number in the NRC is 200543
I have two children
Another is coming
Next summer.
Will you hate him
As you hate me?

*

It is February 2020, and the protests are ebbing, the most fierce pockets of resistance are being put down with ruthlessness. Media attention, always fickle in India, is moving on; most Delhi channels centred the women of Shaheen Bagh but chose to quote only their fears, not their hopes and dreams, not their articulate and fiery vision of a plural and equal land where no citizen is persecuted for their religion. Urdu protest poet Nabiya Khan films a video where she walks silently past walls covered with protest slogans – the poet Faiz Ahmad Faiz's *Hum dekhenge* (We will witness/ We will see this through) among them.

'The revolution will come,' she recites, her voice steady and soaring, 'wearing bindis and bangles, wearing burqa and hijab.' And you remember the words of another poet, Iqra Khilji – *Dharti to yeh Gulzar hai; pairon tale angaar hai* (Our land might seem to be in bloom but there are burning embers under our feet).

You and a few other women help each other scramble to safety at a quiet gathering, far from the media glare at Shaheen Bagh. They were discussing the impact of the laws and the growth of detention centres, when the meeting was violently disrupted by men who pulled down the tents and tore up printouts of the Constitution, who kicked seated, elderly women in the face as the police silently watched.

One woman in her seventies passes around spare gamchas (thin, coarse cotton towels) so that others can bind up their wounds.

She says, 'People ask, what use is all your singing and protests against this hate? But hate can only shatter the country into a thousand pieces. I believe in our songs of freedom and of love. I believe we will sing the country whole, one song at a time.'

Spoken poem in a bottle

Where Does the Sky Come From?

Devangana Kalita and Natasha Narwal

One evening, as we sat gazing at the clouds and the big kites in the sky outside our prison ward, L, an insanely adorable three-year-old child, asked perplexed, '*Aasman kahan se aata hai? Aasman ghar se aata hai kya*?' (Where does the sky come from? Does the sky come from its home?) An innocent, inquisitive question which, in any other context, would have made us laugh; in the space that we found ourselves in, it rattled and broke our hearts. L had been in prison with his mother for almost two years. We got to meet him while we spent nearly thirteen months (from May 2020 to June 2021) in Tihar Jail in Delhi under 'terror' charges for participating in protests against the Citizenship Amendment Act. L's question shook us like no question from the harrowing police interrogation could. The universe and the home – two places that the children imprisoned with their mothers had never known. How does one explain to a kid who has never seen the outside world, who has never seen a starry night sky, that there is a whole universe out there; that there are homes we love and hate outside these prison walls?

The prison, inherently linked to all structures of oppression and exploitation that we find in our societies, is exceptional in the impunity with which it incarcerates primarily the marginalised and takes away all autonomy and dignity. As activists from Pinjra Tod (Break the Cage), a women's collective that has struggled against various forms of oppression that imprison women, the irony of being literally put in a cage was not lost on us. In those thirteen months of prison time, the bonds that gradually developed with our fellow women prisoners and their children helped us survive the brutal incarceration. It was a deeply humbling experience to learn from our fellow inmates, even while struggling everyday against a deeply dehumanising and violent space, how it is possible to retain our humanity and dignity, to create spaces of joy and laughter, to nurture relationships of love and caring created by this collective experience of helplessness and waiting – an affirmation that life happens and can survive in the most brutal situations and places.

In the context of the pandemic, the basic minimal contact with the outside world that was earlier allowed to prisoners in the form of court visits, family interviews (mulaqaats), access to letters and newspapers was suspended for several months. The prisoners only had each other to hold through moments of extreme despair and uncertainty, through what had become an even more intensified form of confinement. With any movement inside the prison premises severely curtailed, 'intermixing' between wards completely barred, and most recreational activities stopped, inmates who had been in prison for years often remarked, '*Ab jail jail lagne laga hai*' (Now jail really feels like jail). Another practice that was instituted inside the prison in response to the pandemic was to put every new prisoner, any prisoner returning from outside (court/hospital visit), and any prisoner who showed symptoms of illness (cough, cold, fever, etc.) into quarantine inside a cell, which meant that they would be locked in, mostly alone, 24/7 for fourteen whole days and no one would be allowed to talk to them even from afar, while they were kept in isolation. In fact, for some inmates with medical issues that required frequent hospital visits, it meant being in a permanent state of quarantine confinement. The days and nights in the isolation cells were immensely terrifying for all of us, the kind of mental trauma and fear it produced led to multiple suicide attempts by different prisoners inside these cells. Little children too would be locked in like this with their mothers, and the children would relentlessly scream '*kholo, kholo*' (open, open) and cry so loud that sometimes you felt the walls would explode.

Encountering and befriending the children inside the prison made the brutality of the incarceration even more stark. Their cries, their questions and attempts at understanding their confinement and ways of being in it, as well as their curiosity about the world outside those walls, one being an everyday lived reality, the other an enigma, but both incomprehensible to them. What does incarceration do to these children's psyches? How do they even make sense of it? What scars does it leave? These are questions still with us and we grapple with them everyday as we struggle to cope with, and understand, our own prison and post-prison lives.

At some point, L realised that there is a world 'outside' to which he must find his way out. There was an urgency to his quest: he began crying a lot more, often for what seemed like no reason at all. Mimicking the male construction workers who would every now and then break down some structure inside prison for repair work, L began to hit the walls, grilles, gates and locks that surrounded our prison ward with anything he could find: sometimes it was a badminton racket, sometimes a plastic cricket bat, sometimes an empty shampoo bottle, sometimes a stone, sometimes just his bare hands. On being asked what he was up to, bang would come a non-nonchalant response: '*Mai jail tod raha hoon'* (I am breaking the prison).

But L, like all the other kids, was also mortally scared of the figure of the 'uncle', which for the kids was embodied in the male policemen who would accompany the workers inside the women's prison for work related to maintenance. This fear was also mixed with an intense curiosity. They would bug us to take them to see the uncle, yet would be mortified as soon as an uncle appeared close by. Rather dramatically, they would start screaming and howling, desperately running around to hide behind any inmate they could find, each time they encountered an uncle. Was it just the fear evoked by a figure they were not familiar with, or was it a fear of 'authority'? Such behaviour intensified after the children witnessed an incident of violence that took place during our initial days in prison, while we were in quarantine. Our fellow inmates told us how male policemen and prison officials had mercilessly beaten up many African inmates for demanding their right to interim bail during the pandemic, which certain Indian inmates had been granted. The little beings had seen blood from cracked skulls, broken arms and limbs, blood that their mothers had been brought in to wipe clean. When his mother got interim bail and L developed some understanding that he would be leaving soon, he came to our barrack, and grasping our hands pleaded, '*Aap mere saath chaloge?'* (Will you come with me?) When we asked him why, he replied pensively, '*Mujhe dar lagta hai. Uncle honge wahan'* (I feel scared. Uncles will be there).

The figures of authority that they so feared were also what they sought to mimic, internalising the everyday life they observed and, of course, lived. One of their favourite games was 'searching'. When a metal detector was installed in the common area, it was the most exciting object in their lives for quite a while – they would press the buttons around it, and walk through it with objects that would make the machine beep. Then there was the 'injection' game, where they would pretend to be the medical assistants who came to collect prisoners' blood samples or give them various vaccines. The first words the children learnt to scream aloud were '*Andar chalo*' (Go inside) and '*Ginti bandh ho rahi hai*' (time for lock up) as they walked around pretending to be either matrons or munshis (convict-warder) of the wards. They would be fascinated by all the locks in the barracks and on the gates and would run behind matrons, wanting to play with their bundles of keys. M, the two-year-old kid of a Brazilian woman prisoner, would repeatedly yell, '*Maarunga danda se*' (I will hit you with a stick) at whoever would not listen to him or whenever he was upset about something.

These children had committed no 'crime', but found themselves in prison because their mothers, often abandoned by their families, had no one in the outside world to whom they could entrust the responsibility of caring for their children while they served prison time. Their mothers were very young, primarily coming from the most marginalised communities in the country,[13] as much prisoners of various forms of structural oppression and exploitation as of situations that may or may not have led them to commit the 'crimes' they stood accused of. They, with other women prisoners, collectively brought up the children, slogging for hours doing various odd jobs inside the prison that did not even pay the basic minimum wage. The money they earned was used for buying a few clothes, milk, food and other supplies for their children from the jail shop.

Most of these women languish in jails for painfully long periods of time, sometimes with no knowledge of the charges against them, the excruciatingly slow and overburdened government legal-aid system being their only access to any remote possibility of justice. Again, the most astounding and heartbreaking demonstration of this criminal justice system where justice is ever-elusive, was provided by the children. A, a two-year-old girl, had gone to court for the first time with her mother. When she returned to the prison, we asked her what she had seen and done. She named many things, and one of them was the judge. When we asked her, 'What does the judge do?', she thought deeply for a minute and responded, '*Kuch bhi nahi karta hai*' (He doesn't do anything).

13. https://indianexpress.com/article/india/ncrb-data-higher-share-of-dalits-tribals-muslims-in-prison-than-numbers-outside-6575446//.

It was quite common to hear the slightly older kids very matter-of-factly ask each other, 'Did your mother get bail? What case is she in?' They packed their bags stitched from old clothes and pretended to leave for court or exclaimed that their '*rihai*' (release) had arrived, that they were going home that night. But release was nowhere in sight. Especially for children like M, whose Brazilian mother, not understanding the language or the court proceedings, ended up pleading guilty to charges on the promise of being sent back to her home country. That promise, however, remains stuck in endless bureaucratic files in different government offices and embassies. The first time M sees the world outside the prison walls will be when he is taken in an aircraft or ship with his mother when the bilateral agreement that permits a transfer of prisoners between the two countries finally comes through.

These children, who had completely captured our very beings, defining our prison time in the most incredible and painful ways, have been an enduring presence in our dreams ever since we got out on bail. Coming to terms with the separation from them, with no possibility of any contact in the near future, has been a deeply destabilising and difficult experience. In one such dream, one of us met M. He had finally been reunited with his grandmother and his other siblings in Rio de Janeiro after many, many years. Older and wiser, standing in front of the sea for the first time, he lets out a shattering scream.

That scream should haunt us all.

Distance between two tears

Prison Diaries

Umar Khalid

17 January 2022

On a cold February morning earlier this year, I was taken out from jail in a police van for my first peshi (presentation) in court, since my arrest in September last year. Inside the van, the cops were having an animated conversation about the farmers' protests. But after four months of captivity, the sight outside was more alluring for me. I could see people going to their offices and children to their schools. There were people in cars, buses and on roads. Some were immersed in their phones, while others were talking to each other. There was no one watching over them. They were free to go wherever, talk to whomever.

It was a fascinating sight – the sight of free people. I was reminded of the past when I too, like the people I was staring at, had been free. The words of Iqbal came to me:

Aata hai yaad mujhko guzra hua zamana
Wo baghon ki baharein, wo sab ka chehchahana
Azaadiyan kahan wo ab apne ghosle ki
Apni khushi se aana apni khushi se jana

I had eagerly waited for this day. Till then, owing to COVID guidelines, all our court proceedings had been held virtually from within the jail itself. Shut out from the outside world in the same physical space for several months, I was feeling trapped. I desperately needed some change.

I think the journey to the court lasted an hour and a half. In court, the proceedings barely lasted thirty minutes. Once the tarikh (date) was over, I was put back in the van for our return journey to jail. All through the journey to court and back, I kept staring outside in amazement, as if I were a tourist being taken on a bus ride of a city that was foreign to me.

By 2 p.m., I had been brought back to Tihar and locked up in my cell soon after. The 'excursion' to the court seemed to have gotten over like those childhood picnics – in no time. Now it was back to the same suffocating and monotonous life within the high walls of Tihar.

*

When I entered Tihar back in September 2020, the first thing that struck me was an eerie stillness. Anybody who has ever been inside the complex will tell you about this eerie stillness. It seemed as if we had entered a ghost town, surrounded by high walls on all sides. As the police car that was shifting me from police station to jail kept moving inside, the sounds of the outside world slowly started to recede and were overtaken by silence.

We had entered the Tihar complex, but were yet to reach the jail where I was to be lodged. Tihar is a huge structure, the biggest prison in South Asia divided into nine different jails. The car kept driving on a totally isolated road before we reached Central Jail No. 2. It was here that the cops were to hand me over to the prison authorities.

But first, some formalities had to be completed. I stood in a line behind others who were also entering the jail that day, waiting for my turn at a window. Behind it, sat a clerk filling up details.

'Naam? Baap ka naam? Kis case mein aaye ho?'

After telling him my name and my father's name, to his last question, I replied 'UAPA'. He had never heard it before, so he thought I had not understood his question.

'*Nahin kaun si dhara lagi hai*?'

'UAPA.'

'*Kya*? *Dhang se batao*?' He was now visibly impatient.

Now the constable of the Delhi Police, who had come to deposit me to jail, replied from behind, '*Dange ke case mein Sir, Delhi danga*.'

The clerk entered it in his register, while looking irritated with me for not having replied properly earlier. It had been eleven days since my arrest, but till this moment, no one had referred to me directly like that. After all these years of speaking out against a politics that thrives on riots, hate and division, I was now entering jail with a slip in my hand that said 'Delhi danga' next to the section for charges. It seemed like someone had punched me really hard in the guts.

But this was no time for sentimentalities, as more immediate fears – formed on the basis of what I had heard about jails – ran through my mind. Where would the jailers keep me? I had heard about the dreaded 'blade-daaz' in jail, those who cut and slash you with blades if you don't give in to their demands. Would they catch hold of me and make their demands – which could range from monetary to sexual? Would I be mistreated in jail due to how the media had portrayed me before my arrest?

Thankfully, nothing like that happened. Instead, jail authorities took special measures to ensure no harm came to me. In the jail premises, I was 'highlight matter' – people whose cases were reported in the media. Any harm to such prisoners would also make it to the media, and reflect poorly on the jail administration.

I was lodged in a separate cell, away from other prisoners, and two jail wardens were assigned to me for my security. I realised that the very thing that had led to my arrest – a televised witch-hunt – now ensured me a protective cover inside jail.

But this created new problems for me as I was to realise in the subsequent days. Unlike other prisoners, I was not let out of my cell into the small verandah outside. In the name of security, they would just keep me lodged inside my cell. Many hours of requests would just give me ten–fifteen minutes of air in the open in the entire day. This confinement which continued for three weeks was quite unnerving. In my next court appearance, I raised it in court. The judge summoned the jail superintendent to court and instructed against keeping me caged like that. This gave me three hours every day – two in the morning and one in the evening. It was still far less than the rest, but after three harrowing weeks, it still seemed to be a big relief. A few months later, I negotiated one more hour from the authorities, and then some months later, some more.

*

Over the past fifteen months, this is what life has been about – daily negotiation for the most basic of things, be it books, warm clothes or just some air in the open. And it has also been wondering about what to do with time, which seems to be in abundance. In his prison memoir, Kenyan writer Ngũgĩ wa Thiong'o writes that contrary to what people think outside, life in jail is not about endless confrontations, it is instead a daily monotony, you wake up, you eat, you defecate, you sleep. Day after day after day. To that, I could add reading, and that pretty much sums up my days and nights over the last fifteen months.

And then one does not know for how long this will last. It is often said that jails are for convicts and not undertrials. But here, I have spent over fifteen months in pre-trial detention. Even now, I can't see our trial commencing anytime soon.

In his memoir, Ngũgĩ wa Thiong'o also talks about this peculiar predicament that political prisoners face – not knowing how long you have to wait till you are free again. In one sense, this makes our situation even worse than that of convicts. They know the length of their situation, and even if it is long, they can prepare themselves mentally for it. On the other hand, we just don't know. We could be free in a month's time or in a year or it may even take ten years.

This uncertainty, which keeps us hanging in a state of animated suspension between hope and hopelessness, is especially difficult to cope with. You always remain hopeful that some judge will see through the absurdity of the charges, and set you free. At the same time, you keep cautioning yourself about the perils of nurturing such hopes. The higher your hopes, the higher would be the height from which you would come crashing down.

*

The functioning and structure of jails, with frequent transfers of inmates and extended periods of isolation, also prevent the building of any meaningful ties with others. Due to this, jail is also an inexplicably lonely and impersonal experience. Even though you are living amid hundreds of other prisoners, you still feel lonely because you are separated from your loved ones. But certain experiences leave me lonelier even amidst prisoners – I am talking about the internalised prejudice and bigotry against Muslims. In jail, I have come face to face with bigotry and prejudice against Muslims unlike anything I have faced before.

A person left me bewildered by asking in front of several people out of nowhere – 'You see all of us as kafirs na?' After the recent India–Pakistan cricket match in the T20 World Cup, another said: *'Arey, kal toh tumhari team ne hamari team ko hara diya.'* More than once, I've been asked how many wives my father has, or how many I intend to have. If they feel you have taken offence, pat comes a defence, *'Arey kya galat bola, aap logo mein toh aise hi hota hai na.'*

I have also realised that a Muslim is always seen as part of one large national, or rather a transnational, group.

He is bereft of any individuality. So many questions posed to him or remarks passed at him are not about him, but about 'aap log' – you people.

'Arey aap logo mein to aisa hota hai, na?'

'Aap kyun Owaisi ke baare mien kuch nahi bolte?'

'Yeh aap logo ne kya kar diya Afghanistan mein?'

None of the above comments that I have faced at different times, have come from consciously hateful people, or from people for whom hate is a political agenda. Instead, they come from ordinary and otherwise 'nice' people, people who come and share their food with you, who tell you their stories of how they landed in jail and ask for your advice on legal matters. And then, talking about the news of the day, will slip into something like this:

'You can't deny Khalid bhai, Muslims support the Pakistani cricket team when they play against India.'

'How many Muslims do you know in your life who support Pakistan?' I ask back.

'I do not know any Muslims in my life, but I know they support Pakistan.'

The prejudice is so deeply ingrained that they believe they are speaking the obvious truth.

And it also comes with such moral righteousness that makes any argument extremely difficult after a while. You simply retreat into silence. Is this where the 'tryst with destiny' was to bring us after seventy years? Are these the destiny's children?

It is not that I am discovering prejudice, bigotry or even hate for the first time. Over the last five years, the regime and its pied pipers in media have constantly reminded me of my 'Muslimness' and also of the place of Muslims in 'New India'. But till now, hate came from a distance, usually from TV and mobile screens. I always had the option of switching it off, if it got too much. My immediate circle – the people I spent time with in real life – sheltered me from hate.

Jail has removed this distance. Now hate and prejudice are up close and in my face. There is nobody to shelter me, and nobody to confide in.

In my long hours of silence and an otherwise apocalyptic solitude, I keep telling myself not to turn bitter about my circumstances. It is quite easy to succumb to bitterness. But bitterness would not leave me good for anything productive, certainly not for the fight we have set out to fight – of reclaiming our country from the forces of hate and divisions. I also keep telling myself to look at the larger perspective.

A friend recently told me the story of a human rights lawyer in Chile who, all through the years of Pinochet, kept fighting cases against him in court. He lost all the cases. But after Pinochet fell, his petitions were used to indict Pinochet for his brutality and crimes against humanity. And now many years later, Chile has elected a left-wing president. So I tell myself – no tyrant lasts forever, he cannot trump the truth and hate can never triumph over love forever.

And on cold starry nights, when I miss my beloved, I find strength in the words of Faiz Ahmad Faiz, written from behind prison bars:

Dil sepaiham khayal kahta hai
itni shirin hai zindagi is pal
zulm ka zahr gholne vaale
kamran ho sakenge aaj na kal
jalva-gah-e-visal ki sham.en
vo bujha bhi chuke agar to kya
chand ko gul karen to ham janen

Though they may concoct tyranny's poisons
They will have no victories,
not today, nor tomorrow.
So what if they douse the flames
in rooms where lovers meet?
If they are so mighty,
let them snuff out the moon.

A note from Chinki Sinha, the Editor of Outlook, *where this text was first published:*

When we decided to go with apocalypse as the theme for Outlook*'s year-ender issue, we knew we had to reach out to Umar Khalid in Tihar Jail. His partner said she would ask him. He said he would write about his days within the prison and that long wait to be heard in the court. Twice, they weren't able to get the piece he had written on paper as jail guards stopped him. The third time, Banjyotsna Lahiri took the sheets in the court, typed it out and sent it to us. This took us more than a month. On 24 December, we received the piece on my WhatsApp. For me, it was the only piece that I had badly wanted. The lines stuck. He had quoted Faiz. It made me believe in love and courage.*

POEMS

For, In Your Tongue, I Cannot Fit

Sound Installation

Tomorrow maybe they will kill us
This smile, and this sky, they cannot take from us.
This smile,
1949, 1967

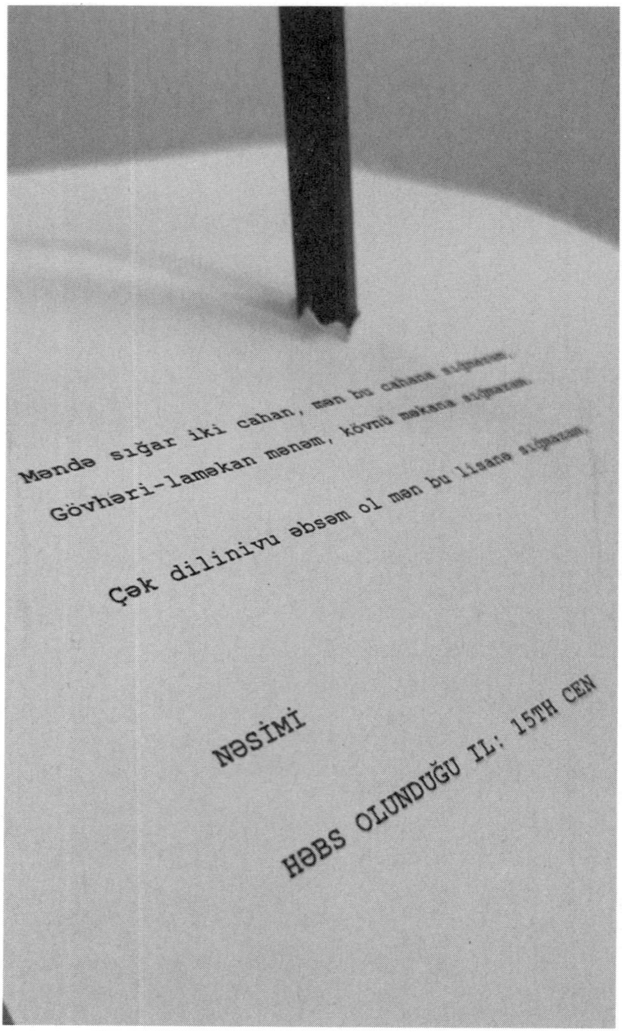
Məndə sığar iki cahan, mən bu cahana sığmazam,
Gövhəri-laməkan mənəm, kövnü məkana sığmazam.
Çək dilinivu əbsəm ol mən bu lisana sığmazam.
NƏSİMİ
HƏBS OLUNDUĞU IL: 15TH CEN

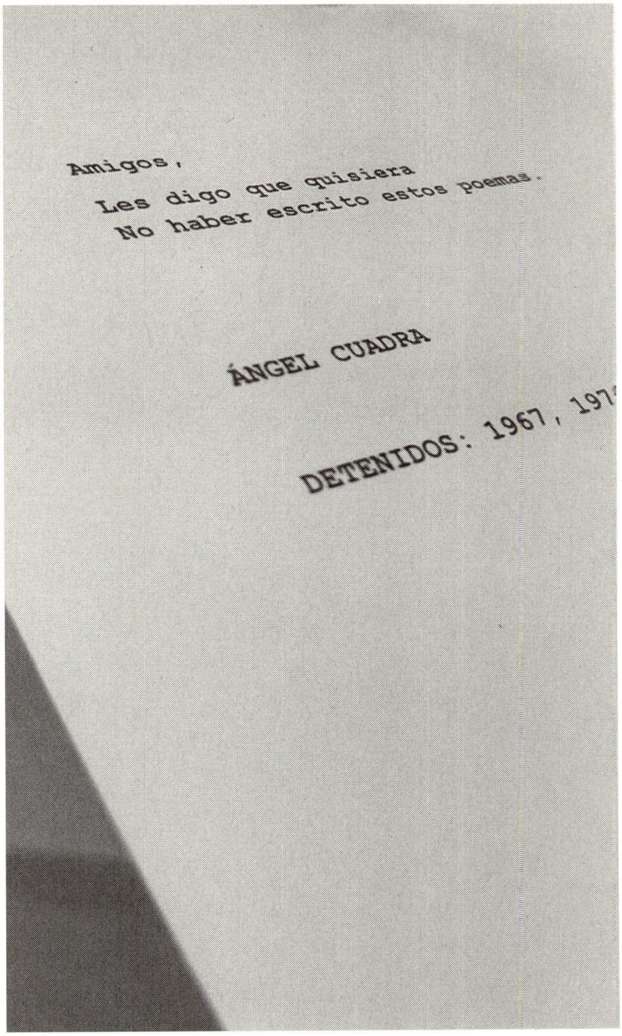
Amigos,
Les digo que quisiera
No haber escrito estos poemas.
ÁNGEL CUADRA
DETENIDOS: 1967, 197

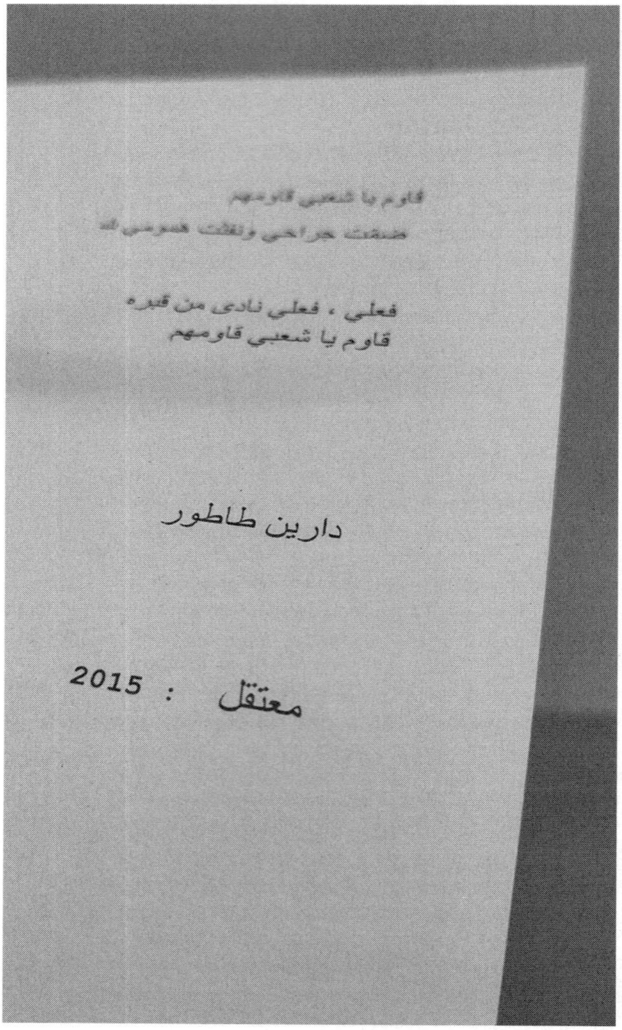
قاوم يا شعبي قاومهم
فعلي ، فعلي نادى من قبره
قاوم يا شعبي قاومهم
دارين طاطور
معتقل : 2015

WOLE SOYINKA
DETAINED: 1967

ऐ मातृभूमि तेरी जय हो, सदा विजय हो।
प्रत्येक भक्त तेरा, सुख-शांति-कान्तिमय हो ।।
वह भक्ति दे कि 'बिस्मिल' सुख में तुझे न भूले,
वह शक्ति दे कि दुःख में कायर न यह हृदय हो ।।
राम प्रसाद बिस्मिल
गिरफ्तार: 1925

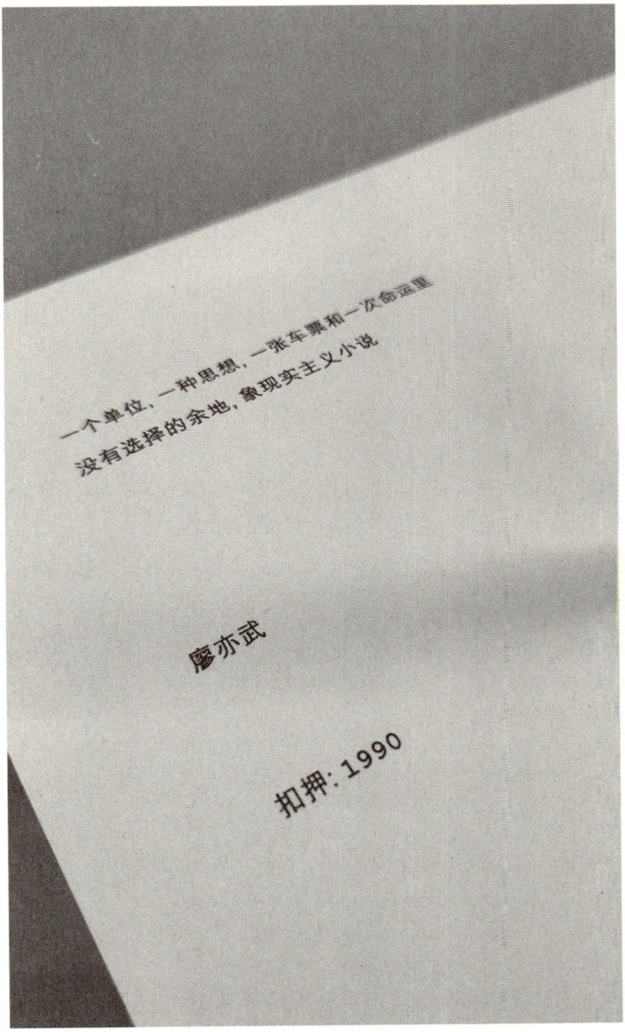
一个单位，一种思想，一张车票和一次命运里
没有选择的余地，象现实主义小说
廖亦武
扣押：1990

Angel Cuadra was born in Havana in 1931 and started composing poetry when he was eight. In 1956, he graduated from the University of Havana with a degree in law and became involved in the anti-Batista movement. In 1953, he read from the steps of Havana University his poem, *A Lament to Jose Marti on His Centenary* (Lamento a Jose Marti en su Centenario), condemning Batista's dictatorship. After the Cuban revolution of 1959, Cuadra's first book of poetry, *Peldaño*, was published, and he worked as a government lawyer. Soon disillusioned with Castro's Cuba, he became active in the anti-communist underground, continuing to publish his poetry in secret. In April 1967, Cuadra was arrested and charged with being an 'enemy of and spreading propaganda about the People's Government'. He was sentenced to fifteen years in prison, but received parole in 1976. He was re-imprisoned a year later when it was found that he had smuggled his poems to the United States. He served out his original sentence and was released in 1982, emigrating to the US in 1985, from where he continued to promote human rights in Cuba and to write poetry, including reflections on his experience in prison.

The Unavoidable Voice

My friends, I say,
I did not want
to have to write these poems.

After so much death
– daily deaths in cells, from anguish, from impotence –
you would have expected from me
a Hymn to Life, a promising song
to raise your spirits.

But I could not,
my friends.

I left the bars behind –
minutes or centuries ago… I cannot tell –
but I still carry the pain of chains,
I am dragging them through the streets.

Streets where I loved years ago,
where I walked with books, with haste,
with fights and with dreams:
with everything that, on my return, I wanted to recover.
But there is only boredom.

I promised myself to shut up.
But I could not, my friends.

These are poems of another truth,
from someone who gathers it and suffers.

And, my friends, I could not
set it behind bars,
in the silence.

Angel Cuadra

Imprisoned: 1967–1982

Translated from Spanish by Luis Ignacio Larcada

For Abu Nuwas

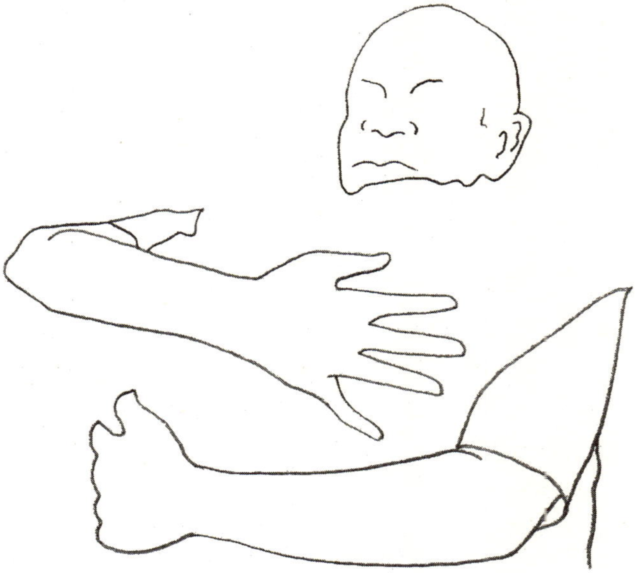

Abu Nuwas was born around 756, in what was then Persia. He was a classical Arab poet, known for a lifestyle that the conservative society despised, and for his homoerotic poetry. Abu Nuwas lived and wrote at a time when homosexuality was openly discussed by Muslim theologians and artists alike, although frowned upon in more conservative circles. With friendships in high places, he was known for his sexual exploits, and for his love of wine. His poems celebrated these in a style that broke with convention and were enjoyed for their indecency, ribaldry and lack of inhibition. His fame was such that he appears as a character in several of the tales in the *Arabian Nights*. Abu Nuwas was imprisoned, possibly twice. The first arrest was for heresy, and the second is believed to have been for satirising the Caliphate in his poetry. There is also a dispute about the manner of his death, around 814, when he was in his late fifties. Some accounts say that he died in prison, while others say that he died of ill-health brought on by his drinking.

A Boy Is Worth More Than a Girl

For young boys, the girls I've left behind
And for old wine set clear water out of mind.
Far from the straight road, I took without conceit
The winding way of sin, because this horse
Has cut the reins without remorse,
And carried away the bridle and the bit.

Here I am, fallen for a faun,
A dandy who butchers Arabic.
His forehead, brilliant like a full moon,
Chases away the black night's gloom.
He cares not for shirts of cotton
Nor for the Bedouin's hair coat.

He sports a short tunic over his slender thighs
but his shirt is long of sleeve.
His feet are well-shod, and under his coat
You can glimpse rich brocade.

He takes off on campaign and rides to attack
casting arrows and javelins;
He hides the ardor of war, and his
Attitude under fire is magnanimous.

Comparing a young boy to a young girl, I am ignorant.
And yet, how can you mix up some bitch
Who goes in monthly heat
And drops a litter once a year
With him I see on the fly.

How I wish he would come
Return my greeting.
I reveal to him all my thoughts
Without fear of the imam, or of the muezzin.

Abu Nuwas

Imprisoned: Eighth century (exact dates unknown)

Translation from Arabic, attributed to Vincent Mansour Monteil

For twenty-seven years between 1960–1991, poet **Nguyễn Chí Thiện** was a political prisoner in Vietnam. He wrote hundreds of poems that were smuggled out and published abroad while he was still imprisoned. Nguyễn was first arrested in 1960 when, as a substitute teacher, he gave a lesson in which he told students that it was the US that had defeated the Japanese Imperial Army in the Second World War, countering the official position that it had been the Soviet Union. He was imprisoned for more than three years, during which he wrote over a hundred poems that he memorised and then circulated clandestinely on his release. When these poems were discovered in 1966, Nguyễn was imprisoned again, then temporarily released in 1977. Seizing the opportunity of brief freedom, in 1979, Nguyễn went to the British embassy in Hanoi, handing over 400 poems and asking that they be published abroad. He was rearrested as he left the embassy and imprisoned for a further twelve years before being released in 1991. The embassy did as Nguyễn requested, and his collection of poems, *Flowers from Hell*, was published in the US in 1984. He continued to write poetry while in exile in the US.

My Mother

My mother on anniversaries or festival days
Is wont to put her hands together and pray for a long time
Her old saffron dress has somewhat faded
But I would see her take it out for the occasion
My life being full of suffering and injustice
Mother always has to pray for me
A son who has seen a number of jail terms
Causing tears to flow in streams on Mother's cheeks.
Sitting next to her, I find myself so small
Next to the great vast love of my mother.
Mother, I only have one real wish
And that is, never to be far away from you!
Now each time that you sit in prayer
For your sick prisoner son in the deep jungle
The old, fading saffron dress you wear
Must be soaked with tears unending!

Nguyễn Chí Thiện

Imprisoned: 1960–1964, 1966–1977, 1979–1991

Translated from Vietnamese by Nguyen Ngoc Bich

French poet, novelist and playwright **Jean Richepin** was imprisoned and fined in 1876 for 'affront to morality' for his poems using street-slang. Until he was brought to court for his collection of verses, *The Beggars' Song* (La Chanson des Gueux), Richepin, then in his late twenties, had been a relatively unknown writer. The case brought him unexpected fame. A public that had become tired of the decorum of the previous generation of poets, found his use of coarse language and vernacular to represent refreshing change, and hailed him as a martyr for freedom of expression. At his trial, Richepin argued that his poetry was a legitimate criticism of social conditions at the time. He was jailed for a month and had to pay a fine of 500 francs. The publisher and printer of the book were also fined. Richepin went on to have a successful career, publishing three more collections of poems, novels and popular plays, many continuing the use of violent language. He was never again brought to court. In his later years, Richepin turned to work on the stage and with opera composers.

The Beggars' Song

It's true that he's coming, let it be sung!
But not on a clear ivory horn,
By those whose icy throat is stung
By winter with its nails like thorns.
Weary! with a stifled wheeze
He is greeted every year by those
Who, on his arrival, freeze,
By those who have no hearth.

He appears, with a hale look,
More joyful than a rising sun,
Bringing gaiety to the inglenook,
With sweets and toys bestowed upon
The rich, triumphant baby.
But what a sad and bitter day
For the poor who feast on wind,
For those who have no hearth!

Blessed is the dear child who prays,
With his shoe with the puffy knot,
For Jesus to smile at him on this day!
But fate to beggars grants it not.

Where to place, in what shining ash,
Their hard shoe, often holey,
What hope to come, which dreams abashed
For those who have no hearth?

Prince, have mercy on those
Whose faces are like parchment.
Make Christmas by warming the toes
Of those who have no hearth.

Jean Richepin

Imprisoned: 1876

Translated from French

Jack Mapanje

Born in Malawi in 1944, **Jack Mapanje** examines exile, imprisonment and political power through his work. He studied in England before returning in 1975 to teach English at the University of Malawi, rising to head its Department of Literature. In 1981, his poetry collection, *Of Chameleons and Gods*, was published in Britain. However, the authorities reacted unfavourably when it was reprinted in 1984. They objected to its oblique criticism of the repressive regime of President Hastings Kazuma Banda. Mapanje was arrested two years later, in 1987, and imprisoned in Mikuyu Prison where he lived under appalling conditions until his release almost four years later. He was never charged or brought to trial. Mapanje says it is impossible to tell why he was imprisoned, but believes it was for his writings and that his poem *Making Our Clowns Martyrs* could have drawn the ire of the authorities for its mockery of government officials. Soon after his release in 1991, on hearing that his life was under threat, Mapanje fled to Britain, where he continues to write and publish poetry.

Making Our Clowns Martyrs
(or Returning Home Without Chauffeurs)

We all know why you have come back home with no
National colours flanking your black Mercedes Benz.
The radio said the toilets in the banquet halls of
Your dream have grown green creepers and cockroaches
Which won't flush, and the orders you once shouted
To the concubines so mute have now locked you in.
Hard luck my friend. But we all know what currents
Have stroked your temper. You come from a breed of
Toxic frogs croaking beside the smoking marshes of
River Shire, and the first words you breathed were
Snapped by the lethal mosquitoes of this morass.
We knew you would wade your way through the arena
Though we wondered how you got chosen for the Benz.
You should have been born up the hills, brother where
Lake waters swirl and tempers deepen with each season
Of the rains. There you'd see how the leopards of
Dedza hills comb the land or hedge before their assault.
But welcome back to the broken reed-fences, brother;
Welcome home to the poached reed-huts you left behind;
Welcome to these stunted pit-latrines where only
The pungent whiff of buzzing flies gives way.
You will find your idle ducks still shuffle and fart
In large amounts. The black dog you left still sniffs
Distant recognition, lying, licking its leg-wounds. And
Should the relatives greet you with nervous curiosity
In the manner caved in somebody's image,
There is always across the dusty road, your mad auntie.
She alone thinks this new world is going shit. She
Alone still cracks about why where whys are crimes!

Jack Mapanje

Imprisoned: 1987–1991

Thought to have been born in Azerbaijan around 1369, **Imadeddin Nesimi** came to prominence for his poems, which were passionate depictions of emotional and spiritual love. He wrote in Persian and Azeri, publishing one diwan (collection) in each language, and also in Arabic. Nesimi was an ardent follower of Fazlullah Astarabadi, the leader of the Hurufi sect, and spread his beliefs through his poems. At the centre of Hurufisim, of Sufi origin, is 'letter symbolism', where each letter of the alphabet represents an aspect of human nature, and all, taken together, can be seen to represent God. Man is considered to be an incarnation of God. Astarabadi was denounced as a heretic and executed. Nesimi was similarly condemned and executed in Aleppo, Syria, fifteen years later, in 1417. Nesimi's execution by flaying has given rise to many myths. One is that as he was dying, he mocked his executioners in verse. His writings remained influential in the centuries that followed. He is celebrated in modern-day Azerbaijan, and his tomb in Aleppo is a pilgrimage site.

Both Worlds Can Fit Within Me

Both worlds can fit within me, but in this world I cannot fit
I am the essence, I have no place, but into existence I cannot fit

All that was, is and will be, everything is embodied in me,
Do not ask! Come with me. In explanations I cannot fit.

The Universe is my verse; my instance is your life.
Recognize me by these signs; know that in signs I cannot fit.

Through assumption and doubt no truth was found
He who learned the truth knows that in guess I cannot fit.

Look deeper into my form and try to understand the meaning
I am the body and the soul, in my soul with body I cannot fit.

I am the jewel, hidden in shell. I am the bridge that leads to heaven and hell.
With such a wealth, in markets of this world I cannot fit.
...

I am the stars, I am the planets, and the angel of revelation
Hide your tongue, for in your tongue I cannot fit.

I am a particle of all things, I am the sun, and I am the six sides of your land.
Look at me with clarity, because in clarity I cannot fit.

I am at once the essence and the character, I am the sugar with the flower,
I am the decision and the excuse, in silent mouth I cannot fit.

I am a tree on fire; I am the spinning wheel.
Admire the flames of my fire, in these flames I cannot fit.

I am the sweet dream, the moon and the sun. The breath, the soul, I give.
But even in the soul and breath I cannot fit.

I am the arrow and I am the bow, I am the young and I am the old,
I am the power and eternal wealth, but the ages I cannot fit.

Although today I am Nesimi, a Hashemi and a Quareishi
I am less than my glory is, but in my glory I cannot fit.

Imadeddin Nesimi

Executed: 1417

Translated from Azeri

Under house arrest.
Allowed outside movement only
under supervision by her brother.

Dareen Tatour

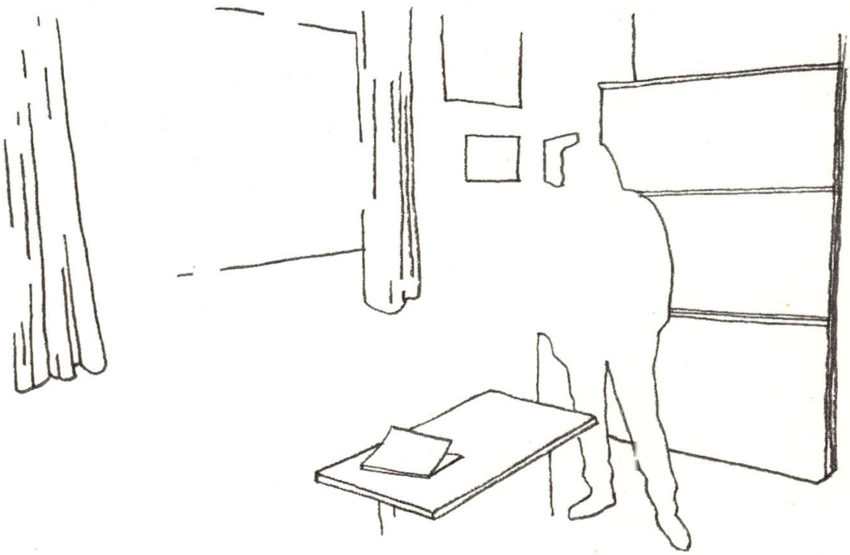

Dareen Tatour, a Palestinian poet in Israel, spent three years between 2015 and 2018 under spells of house arrest and imprisonment. She was convicted of inciting violence and terrorism for a poem she had published on YouTube, *Resist, My People, Resist Them* (Qawem Ya Shaabi Qawemahum). Tatour writes in Arabic and when her case came to trial, it raised long debates on whether the texts that were translated into Hebrew by the police had been rendered accurately or if they were deliberately distorted and misrepresented. These included the words 'martyr' and 'intifada', which the prosecution interpreted as calls to violence, but experts who testified said had been misconstrued and distorted to make it appear as though the terms were extremist and violent. When arrested, Tatour was thirty-three, and her trial dragged on until May 2018, when she was given a five-month prison sentence, reduced to three months for time already served, not taking into consideration the fact that she had been in and out of house arrest for three years, of which nine months were far away from her home near Nazareth. Soon after her release in September 2018, Tatour left for Sweden where she took up an International Cities of Refuge Network residency.

Resist, My People, Resist Them

In my Quds I dressed my wounds,
Recounted my sorrows to God
And put my soul in my palm
For an Arab Palestine,
I will not agree to a peace solution
As long as the poison is spreading
And killing flowers from my country.

I will never lower my flags
Until I take them out of my homeland,
I will defeat them when the time comes.
Resist them, my people, resist,
Resist the settler's greed,
Shred the shameful constitution
Which carried the depressing humiliation
And prevented us from reclaiming our rights.

Resist them, my people, resist
And follow the caravan of martyrs.
They burned the innocent children
And they sniped at Hadil in public,
Murdered her in broad daylight.
They plucked Muhammad's eyes.
Crucified him and drew pain on his body.
They poured hatred on Ali,
Set fire
And burned hopes in a cradle.
Resist the Mista'arev's evil
And do not listen to the collaborators
Who tied us to the illusion of peace,
Do not fear the fire tongues of the Merkava tank
For the belief in your heart is stronger
As long as you resist in a homeland
Which experienced invasions and did tire,
For Ali is calling from his grave.
Resist, my rebellious people.
Write me as parts of the incense branch
And you became the response to my remains.

Dareen Tatour

Imprisoned and house arrest: 2015–2018

Translated from Arabic by Terrie Dawood

In 1989, China was convulsed with protests as students and workers demanded democratic rights. The government responded with force, and thousands died during the crackdown at Tiananmen Square and elsewhere. **Liao Yiwu**'s poem *Massacre* is a visceral condemnation of the episode. For this, he was imprisoned for four years, followed by ostracisation, and then exile. The authorities favoured Liao in his early years, and he was a State-employed writer. This changed in 1989, when two of his poems, *The Yellow City* and *Idol*, which lashed out against government repression, led to his arrest. Knowing that it would rouse the government into taking action, Liao recorded on audiotape *Massacre*, a stream of consciousness cry against the Tiananmen events, that was circulated underground. He was arrested in 1990, and spent four years in prison, during which time he suffered torture and mental breakdowns. Yet, while there, his interviews with inmates inspired him to write *Corpse Walker: Real Stories from the Bottom Up*, which comprised tales of people from the margins of the society. After his release, Liao lived under constant surveillance and harassment. Though published abroad, his writings were banned in China and he was stopped from travelling overseas when invited to speak at events. Eventually, in 2011, he left China, finding asylum in Germany, where he continues to live and write.

Massacre

(Composed on the morning of 4 June 1989)
Dedicated to those who were killed on that day
Dedicated to the two hundredth anniversary of the French Revolution

Leap! Howl! Fly! Run!
Freedom feels so good!
Snuffing out freedom feels so good!
Power will be triumphant forever.
Will be passed down from generation to generation forever.
Freedom will also come back from the dead.
It will come back to life in generation after generation.
Like that dim light just before the dawn.
No. There's no light.
At Utopia's core there can never be light.
Our hearts are pitch black.
Black and scalding.
Like a corpse incinerator.
A trace of the phantoms of the burned dead.
We will exist.
The government that dominates us will exist.
Daylight comes quickly.
It feels so good.
The butchers are still ranting!
Children. Children, your bodies all cold.
Children, your hands grasping stones.
Let's go home.
Brothers and sisters, your shattered bodies littering the earth.
Let's go home.
We walk noiselessly.
Walk three feet above the ground.
All the time forward, there must be a place to rest.
There must be a place where sounds of gunfire and explosions cannot be heard.
We so wish to hide within a stalk of grass.
A leaf.
Uncle. Auntie. Grandpa. Granny. Daddy. Mummy.
How much farther till we're home?
We have no home.
Everyone knows.
Chinese people have no home.
Home is a comforting desire.
Let us die in this desire.
OPEN FIRE, BLAST AWAY, FIRE!

Let us die in freedom.
Righteousness. Equality. Universal love.
Peace, in these vague desires.
Stand on the horizon.
Attract more of the living to death!
It rains.
Don't know if it is rain or transparent ashes.
Run quickly, Mummy!
Run quickly, son!
Run quickly, elder brother!
Run quickly, little brother!
The butchers will not let up.
An even more terrifying day is approaching.
OPEN FIRE! BLAST AWAY! FIRE! IT FEELS GOOD! FEELS SO GOOD! . . .
Cry cry cry crycrycrycrycrycrycry
We stand in the midst of brilliance but all people are blind.
We stand on a great road but no one is able to walk.
We stand in the midst of a cacophony but all are mute.
We stand in the midst of heat and thirst but all refuse to drink.
In this historically unprecedented massacre only the spawn of dogs can survive.

Liao Yiwu

Imprisoned: 1990–1994

Translated from Chinese by Michael M. Day

Dennis Brutus was an anti-apartheid campaigner. Born in Rhodesia, now Zimbabwe, in 1924, Brutus worked as a teacher in South Africa. His anti-apartheid activities focussed on lobbying the IOC to bar South Africa from the Games for excluding non-White athletes from its team. Banned from teaching and political activities in 1961, Brutus was arrested in 1963 as he attempted to meet with the IOC. He escaped while on bail, was rearrested, and when he made a second escape bid, he was shot in the back. He spent sixteen months on the infamous Robben Island before being released, first into exile in Britain, before going on to teach African literature at universities in the US. It was while he was in prison that he learned that South Africa had been expelled from the Olympics; the country could return to the games only in 1992, after apartheid ended. In 1964, Brutus's first collection of poems, written in prison, was published. He went on to publish around a dozen books of poetry exposing the brutal oppression under apartheid. He eventually returned to South Africa, where he died in 2009.

Somehow We Survive

Somehow we survive
and tenderness, frustrated, does not wither.

Investigating searchlights rake
our naked unprotected contours;

over our heads the monolithic decalogue
of fascist prohibition glowers
and teeters for a catastrophic fall;

boots club the peeling door.

But somehow we survive
severance, deprivation, loss.

Patrols uncoil along the asphalt dark
hissing their menace to our lives,

most cruel, all our land is scarred with terror,
rendered unlovely and unlovable;
sundered are we and all our passionate surrender

but somehow tenderness survives.

Dennis Brutus

Imprisoned: 1963–1964

Ram Prasad Bismil was a freedom fighter and poet who was executed under British colonial rule in India in 1927, when he was thirty. Bismil took up the struggle against British colonialism in 1915, when he was eighteen. He wrote rousing poetry against oppression. In 1918, he formed an armed youth resistance group in Uttar Pradesh, his home region. His poem *Vow of the Manipuris* (Manipuri ki Pratigya) was a call to action. Bismil's group went on to carry out robberies against the British colonialists, the proceeds of which they used to buy arms and equipment. In the first instance in 1919, the Manipuri Conspiracy, they carried out three robberies. Apprehended by the police on the third, Bismil escaped by swimming across a river. He spent two years in hiding, returning when the charges were lifted, to resume revolutionary politics. In 1925, in what was known as the Kakori Conspiracy, his group attempted a heist on a passenger train which was carrying money belonging to the British Army. This time, he was captured. After an eighteen-month trial, he and three others were executed by hanging. Bismil's memory lives on through his writings and his autobiography, written while in prison. He is celebrated as a key figure in India's struggle for independence.

Hail, O Motherland, May Victory Always Be Yours

Hail, O Motherland
May you be always victorious
May your bhaktas all know joy-peace-light

In the night of ignorance
When sorrow reigns in all directions
May your dawn arise in the heart of the world

May your rage mean a deluge, a mahapralaya for the world
May your joy mean the world rejoices

Grant such bhakti that 'Bismil'
Does not forget you in his happiness

Grant such strength, O Mother
That this heart knows no cowardice
even in its sorrows

Ram Prasad Bismil

Executed: 1927

Translated from Hindi by Gopika Jadeja

Habib Jalib

Habib Jalib was a revolutionary poet who spent his life using poetry as a tool to expose the abuses of power by Pakistani leaders. He was arrested several times under successive regimes. Jalib was known for his recitation of poems at mushairas, or poetry conclaves, and for his street performances during political demonstrations. One such occasion was in 1983 when he gave recitals in the midst of women protestors, supporting their call to be treated equally before law. He was among those beaten by the police. A member of the Pakistan Communist Party in the 1950s, he was first arrested in 1954 after he recited a poem on the killing of children, and then again in 1959, for reading another of his poems on radio. From then on, he was jailed several times for verses that criticised Gen. Ayub Khan, whose military rule he opposed. He also crossed swords with the government of Zulfiqar Ali Bhutto and the dictatorship of Gen. Muhamad Zia ul-Huq. Prime Minister Benazir Bhutto's government released him in 1988. He died in Lahore in 1993. Jalib's 1962 poem *Constitution* (Dastoor), a protest against military rule, is still cited today during protest movements in South Asia.

Constitution

Those
who illuminate lamps only in palaces
who care only about the chosen few
who thrive in the shadows of compromise
Such empty conventions, such a lustreless dawn
I refuse to know, I refuse to follow

Tell the hangman, I am also Mansoor
A martyr, I am not afraid of his scaffold
Why do you threaten me with prison walls?
Your cruel tyranny, that night of captivity
I refuse to believe, I refuse to claim my own.

The trees are in bloom, you say
The cup runneth over, you say
The gashes on our breasts are healing, you say
These bare lies, this impoverishing of intelligence
I refuse to accept, I refuse to ignore.

For centuries you have plundered our peace
You hold us in your thrall no more
Your claim to be our saviour, our healer
I refuse to acknowledge, I refuse to accept.

Habib Jalib

Imprisoned: Several occasions, 1950s–1980s

Translated from Urdu by Gopika Jadeja

Tsering Woeser is a poet, blogger and journalist from Tibet who writes on Tibetan culture and politics. She is a member of a small group of Tibetans writing in Chinese who have brought Tibetan writing to international attention. She was born in Lhasa in 1966, and grew up speaking Tibetan and Chinese, and studied Chinese literature in Chengdu in Sichuan province. She returned to Tibet to work as a journalist and became editor of the Chinese-language magazine *Tibetan Literature.* She published her first collection of poetry, *Tibet Above* (Xizang Zai Shang), in 1999. Her poem *Remembering a Battered Buddha* is a reflection on the Cultural Revolution's impact on Tibetan culture, one of the themes of her work. Tsering Woeser's writings are banned in China. She has lived in Beijing since 2003. She gets around censorship by publishing her poetry and essays online, and her books are published in Taiwan, which ensures that she is widely read in China and abroad. However, she has lived under constant harassment, including being held under brief periods of house arrest. She has faced interference with, and the blocking of, her social media accounts. She has also been prevented from travelling abroad to receive international awards for her writings and activism.

Remembering a Battered Buddha

Twenty days since I left Lhasa
But still I see that statue of the Buddha with its face bashed in.
It was on a street vendor's stand in front of the Tromsikhang neighborhood office.
I noticed it from a distance.
I'd gone to Tromsikhang Market to buy droma,
But at the sight a sudden grief assailed me.
I drew closer—couldn't help it—to this thing so crushed:
It seemed alive, leaning against a shelf in agony,
The face hammered, an arm hacked off, the whole figure chopped off at the waist.
Hurting so bad, leaning against a rack of the goods
That surrounded it: soy sauce, bean jam, salad dressing, and roll after roll of toilet paper,
All introduced into our life long ago from inland China.
Around its neck an ornament, once exquisite, inlaid with colored stones,
And at its chest a wondrous beast with lion head and body of man,
Stacked on a fragmentary chorten.
In what sacred shrine or pious home were these things once venerated?
Hurting so bad and leaning against the rack of merchandise,
It emanated the calm of still waters, but pain stabbed into my marrow:
As I looked on in grief, I sensed a story being played out
That had both a present and a past.
I was moved by the shadowy fate that had brought us together,
As if melted snow from the high peaks had filled my being.
Hugging his knees, the peddler made a pitch:
'Come on, buy it! Don't the old buddha look grand?'
'When did it get beat up like this?' I asked.
'Cultural Revolution, obviously!' he glanced up, 'Had to be the Cultural Revolution.'
'How much?' I wanted to buy it, to take it home,
But this peddler from Jiangxi wouldn't budge from three thousand.
So with reluctance and regret, and many an afterthought,
I left that broken buddha streaming rays of pain.
I only took some pictures,
So when I miss it I can turn on my computer and have a look.
Friends say it may have been a brand-new buddha, wrecked thus
To fetch a higher price, and the link to the Cultural Revolution was a fiction.
Maybe so; but the hurt remains.
I wrote these lines to try to let it go.

Tsering Woeser

House Arrest: Several occasions since 2008

Translated from Chinese by Andrew E. Clark

Auguste-Marseille Barthélémy was hugely popular for his satirical writings, which slammed the great and the good of early nineteenth-century France. He and his collaborator, Joseph Méry, wrote a series of political satires during the early 1820s, including *L'Villéliade, L'insurrection* and *Napoléon en Egypt.* So popular were these titles that several editions were printed in just one year. Barthélémy came to be known as a 'political chameleon'. His 1825 pro-monarchist poem *Le Sacre de Charles X* earned him the favour of the king's court. But then, in 1829, he published the poem *Son of Man* (Fils de l'homme), a sentimental glorification of Napoleon's son. That led to a three-month prison term and a heavy fine. The press followed the trial closely, and his popularity rose when he delivered his defence entirely in verse. Freed in 1832, he produced more verse satirically ridiculing the government of King Louis Philippe, which he published weekly in the press. Yet, in 1832, a poem supporting the monarchy led to suggestions that he had been silenced in return for a generous pension. He returned to satire in the 1840s but never regained his popularity.

Son of Man

...

Hope brought low to a people calmed,
Grandson of Cesar and son of a King embalmed,
World's inheritor, Emperor at birth,
Today, THE SON OF MAN, hath all your girth—
And yet, what royal child for this obscure name
Would not swap the title and future reign?

...

Auguste-Marseille Barthélémy

Imprisoned: 1829

Translated from French by Jack Cox

Ken Saro-Wiwa was one of Nigeria's most beloved writers and an Ogoni rights and environmental activist. He was executed by hanging on 10 November 1995. Saro-Wiwa's works include *Basi & Co*, a soap opera that ran for 150 episodes. His novel *Soza Boy*, written in pidgin English, is described as one of African literature's finest achievements. His poems include powerful condemnations of war. In the early 1990s, Saro-Wiwa took up the struggle for Ogoni rights. With international oil extraction causing devasting pollution in the Niger Delta, he led a movement that targeted international petroleum companies, calling for an end to human rights abuses and compensation for environmental destruction wrought by oil spills. He was arrested in 1994 and accused of complicity in the murder of four Ogoni chiefs who had been killed during a protest. In November 1995, he and eight others were executed after a trial that was internationally condemned as fraudulent and politically motivated. Eventually, in 2009, accused of complicity in human rights abuses against the Ogoni, Shell, the oil company Saro-Wiwa had campaigned against, paid out a large sum in an out-of-court settlement to Saro Wiwa's family and others. It, however, denied any wrongdoing.

Dance Your Anger and Your Joys

Dance your anger and your joys
Dance the military guns to silence
Dance their dumb laws to the dump
Dance oppression and injustice to death
Dance the end of Shell's ecological war of 30 years
Dance my people for we have seen tomorrow
And there is an Ogoni Star in the sky

Ken Saro-Wiwa

Executed: 1995

In December 2015, **Mehdi Mousavi**, and fellow poet Fatemeh Ekhtesari, left Iran to live in Norway. Two months earlier, they had been sentenced to long prison terms and were to face flogging. Mousavi was born in 1976 and had started writing poetry in the late 1990s. He has published five collections, two of which are banned. He is a leading member of the radical post-modern Ghazal group, that challenges traditional ghazal poetry through the rejection of religious and ideological dogma and a focus on social issues. While the group is banned, there are underground gatherings where works by the group are read and discussed and they are widely available online. Mousavi and Ekhtesari co-edit the banned literary magazine *It Was the Very Tomorrow* (Hamin Fard Bood). They were arrested in December 2013 and held in the notorious Evin Prison for a month until they were granted bail. In October 2015, they were sentenced (Ekhtesari to eleven and a half years in prison and Mousavi to nine years) because an exiled rapper, Shahin Najafi, had used their poetry in his lyrics. The flogging was for acts 'short of adultery': they had shaken hands with members of the opposite sex while on visits abroad.

To Defy Shattering I Petrified Like a Rock

To defy shattering I petrified like a rock.
Now the cranes lift me away.
To a deity that we are not being,
All the reasons are proving what is not.
Deploring a wasted bygone, we wait
For a future modeled after the fossils.
My honor trashes me; my friends and my land, too;
Even they trash me now: my own lines of verse.
A forsaken file in an archive I am;
Come read me out of this layered text.
It was not rain, if my face looks wet.
Not a burden of ordain, but a dagger is in my back.
Stop asking for names, this futile word play!
Cain too, my friend, bore the name of 'brother'.
From infancy onwards, Pain by your side.
Your one and only friend, Pain by your side.
You turned into a poet, for a herd of hogs.
Turned into a poet, but poetry was just pain.

...

Mehdi Mousavi

Sentenced: 2015

Translated from Persian by Amir Khadem

In defense of 'Tar' - a traditional string instrument banned during the Soviet Era.

Mushfig

In 1938, thirty-year-old Azerbaijani poet **Mikayil Mushfig** was executed. He was a victim of Stalin's 'Great Purge'. Azerbaijan was part of the Soviet Union at the time, and Mushfig was a teacher. He started publishing his poetry in his late teens, and in the 1930s was among the group of writers who developed the Azerbaijani Soviet style, which glorified workers, peasants and industrialisation. However, he came into conflict with the authorities in 1936 with his poem *Sing Tar, Sing*, a response to Stalin's edict that traditional Azerbaijani instruments should be replaced by Western ones. The tar is an Azerbaijani lute which Mushfig praised for its ability to portray both joy and mourning. Such was the popular response to Mushfig's poem that the threat to remove traditional instruments was withdrawn. However, in June 1937, Mushfig was arrested and seven months later, on 5 January 1938, he was convicted of treason in a trial that lasted a mere twenty-five minutes. He was executed the following day. Before his arrest, Mushfig had been subject to a slander campaign by other pro-Stalinist writers who had accused him of being 'chauvinist' and 'petit-bourgeois'. Such vitriol between writers under Stalin was not uncommon. After his death, Mushfig's wife and sister were interned, and his brother committed suicide to avoid arrest. All of them, including Mushfig, were exonerated in 1956, three years after Stalin's death.

Sing Tar, Sing

Sing, Tar, sing, Tar, sing!
Verses of beauty go dancing around,
Sing, Tar, sing, Tar, sing!
Dew on my soul is each sweet ringing sound.
Sing, Tar, sing, Tar, sing!
Who can forget you who once heard you sing?
Grief of the people, the tears of their heart—
This is their music, their fiery art.

Buildings that face the kiblah heard your scales,
Everything heard you, the sky and the ground,
Fathers in fur caps and mothers in veils,
Sighed as they listened to each singing sound.
Now it was gladness, now sadness again,
Gaily but warily glided the strain.

...

People are standing about you, a throng,
Waiting to hear the delight of your song:
Workers of factories, women and maids,
Men on the tractors, and hands of all trades!
Sing, there is no one your song- to restrain!
Bitterness, sweetness are part of your strain:
This is the fiery beauty in you—
Art of my native, industrious Baku,
Cotton-fields vast of Ganja—poets' town,
Silk of Sheki, its silk-worms of renown.
Sing, Tar, sing, Tar, sing!
Songs of great beauty go dancing around,
Sing, Tar, let your chords ring!
Dew on the flame of my soul is each sound, I
Sing, Tar, sing, Tar, sing!
Who can forget you who once heard you sing?!
Life of the people, the joy of their heart,
Here is their wonderful, fiery art!

Mikayil Mushfig

Executed: 1938

Translated from Azeri by Olga Moisseyenko

Zeb-un-Nissa

Zeb-un-Nissa was a Mughal princess in India who was held captive by her father for twenty years until she died. She was a gifted and much-loved poet, and her work is still widely read today. It is not clear why Zeb-un-Nissa's father, the Mughal emperor Aurangzeb, turned against her. She had been his most favoured child. Highly intelligent, she studied maths and science under the best tutors, and was fluent in Arabic, Persian and Urdu. She was also a gifted musician and singer. Aurangzeb even sought her advice on political issues. Then, when she was in her forties, he had her imprisoned in the Salimgarh Fort, Delhi, where she died in 1702. The reasons for Aurangzeb's anger are unclear. It may have been because of her affair with a local governor and rival. Some refer to her support for a rival who was fighting to succeed Aurangzeb. It may have been a result of his intolerance of his daughter's writing and musicianship, alongside her interest in Sufiism, which was an anathema to his traditionalist views. She had hidden her poetry from him, giving herself the pen name 'Makhfi' – the Hidden One. Zeb-un-Nissa left an extraordinary legacy of more than 5,000 poems, which were published after her death in the *Diwan-i-Makhfi* (Book of the Hidden One).

Waterfall, Why Are You Lamenting

O waterfall, why are you lamenting?
At whose remembrance did grief wrinkle your face?
What was your pain that all through the night
You kept striking your head on the rocks,
Shedding tears?

...

Zeb-un-Nissa

Imprisoned: 1681–1702

As spoken in Urdu by Shabir – a guide at Lahore Fort – to visiting Indian poet Adil Jussawalla, who wrote it down

Under house arrest.
Liu Xia, wife of Liu Xiaobo

On 10 December 2010, Chinese writer and activist **Liu Xiaobo** was awarded the Nobel Peace Prize. He could not be at the ceremony as he was imprisoned, the first time that the recipient was not present. Liu, a constant critic of the Chinese government, was in and out of prison from 2008 until his death in 2017. His writings were banned. He was first imprisoned between 1989 and 1991 for his involvement in the Tiananmen Square democracy movement. Liu was a professor of literature at Columbia University and had returned to China to be among the protestors. His leading role there led him to be named as one of the 'Black hands of Beijing' by the authorities. He was jailed two more times between 1995 and 1999. Then, in 2008, he was arrested again and sentenced to eleven years in prison for his role in developing and drafting Charter 08, a document reiterating human rights, which grew into a reform movement. His health declined in prison, and he died in hospital while on medical parole in 2017, never regaining his freedom. Throughout, Liu was a prolific writer and his essays and books, although banned in China, were published abroad. Each year, Liu marked the anniversary of the 4 June Tiananmen Massacre with a poem dedicated to those who had died. In 2012, his collection of poems, *June 4th Elegies*, was published in English translation.

Experiencing Death

I had imagined being there beneath sunlight
with the procession of martyrs
using just the one thin bone
to uphold a true conviction
And yet, the heavenly void
will not plate the sacrificed in gold
A pack of wolves well-fed full of corpses
celebrate in the warm noon air
aflood with joy
Faraway place
I've exiled my life to
this place without sun
to flee the era of Christ's birth
I cannot face the blinding vision on the cross
From a wisp of smoke to a little heap of ash
I've drained the drink of the martyrs, sense spring's
about to break into the brocade-brilliance of myriad flowers
Deep in the night, empty road
I'm biking home
I stop at a cigarette stand
A car follows me, crashes over my bicycle
some enormous brutes seize me
I'm handcuffed eyes covered mouth gagged
thrown into a prison van heading nowhere
A blink, a trembling instant passes
to a flash of awareness: I'm still alive
On Central Television News
my name's changed to 'arrested black hand'
though those nameless white bones of the dead
still stand in the forgetting
I lift up high up the self-invented lie
tell everyone how I've experienced death
so that 'black hand' becomes a hero's medal of honor
Even if I know
death's a mysterious unknown
being alive, there's no way to experience death
and once dead
cannot experience death again
yet I'm still
hovering within death
a hovering in drowning

Countless nights behind iron-barred windows
and the graves beneath starlight
have exposed my nightmares
Besides a lie
I own nothing

Liu Xiaobo

Died on medical parole while imprisoned: 2017

Translated from Chinese by Jeffrey Yang

Joseph Brodsky

One of the Arab world's most influential contemporary writers, Ali Ahmad Said Esber is known by his pen name, **Adonis**. He has lived in exile for most of his adult life. In 1955, while doing military service, he was imprisoned in Damascus for being a member of the opposition Syrian National Socialist Party. He was released the following year, and left for exile in Lebanon. There he co-founded two literary journals and went on to publish more than twenty volumes of poetry, books of literary criticism and other works. One of these, an anthology of Arabic poetry, has not been out of print since it was first published in 1964. With the outbreak of the Lebanese Civil War in 1985, Adonis moved to Paris, where has lived since. Adonis is highly regarded for his work, which has been described as experimental and is considered to be an important force in Arab literature. His writing's themes include reflections on exile and on the conflicts in Palestine, Syria and Lebanon. He has been nominated several times for the Nobel Prize in Literature. Adonis's high profile makes him a target for death threats. In recent years, such threats have been made online by religious extremists who consider him an 'infidel' due to his comments on the conflict in Syria.

Time

Hugging the ear of corn
of Time,
my head a tower of fire:
What blood is this that flows across the sand,
what eclipse is this?
Tell us, O, flame of the present,
what shall we say?

The tatters of history fill my larynx
and on my countenance the signs
of the victim.
How bitter language has now become,
and how narrow the door of the alphabet.

Hugging the ear of corn
of Time,
my head a tower of fire:
..../ A friend turned executioner? A neighbour said:
How slow is Hulago? Who is knocking?
A ransom collector?
Give him the dues..
Shapes of women and men...walking images/
We gestured
and exchanged whispers,
our footsteps a string of murder/
Does your murder beget your God
or your God beget your murder?
- The riddle has confused him,
so he bent,
an arch of terror over his drooping days.

- I have lost a brother, my father has gone insane,
and my children have died.
Whose help do I invoke? Do I hug the door?
Complain to a carpet?
- He is dazed; bring the urn and grant him recovery
with the snuff of the Ayatullahs.

...

Adonis

Imprisoned: 1955; exiled: 1956

Translated from Arabic by Kamal Abu-Deeb

Samuel Bamford was a radical social reformer and poet who championed the working class during the upheavals of the British Industrial Revolution. He was a mill worker. He was twice jailed for treason, first in 1817 and then in 1819, for his part in a meeting held in St Peter's Field in Manchester in August, where around 60,000 people had gathered to demand political representation at a time when only wealthy landowners could vote. In what became known as the 'Peterloo Massacre', a sardonic reference to the Battle of Waterloo four years earlier, around eighteen people were killed and many hundreds injured when a private militia cavalry charge, hired by wealthy local businessmen, was ordered to disperse the crowd. Bamford was found guilty of unlawful assembly and imprisoned for a year. His poem, *The Fray of Stockport*, published in his collection *The Weaver Boy* (1819) describes, in rousing vernacular, an incident in 1818, a year before Peterloo, when yeomen were called in to quell another protest. There, the protestors were able to drive back their attackers with sticks and stones.

The Fray of Stockport

HA! han they ta'en our cap and flag;
Wot! han the Dandies ta'en 'em?
An' did Reformers' courage lag,
An' could they not regain 'em?
An' did the Gentles ride so gay,
Wi' Birch and Loyd afore 'em,
To sweep the 'Gruntin herd' away,
Or bravely gallop o'er 'em?

O! wot could stan' afore the might
O' Yeomanry so loyal?
Who came to drive the "herd" aright,
An' would ha' no denial;
Until the stones began to fly,
An' heads began a crackin',
An' then our Gallant Yeomanry
Were fain to find a backin'.

...

Then amblin' up the 'Gemmen' came
Towards the front o'th hustin';
But, soon their folly did they blame,
The 'rabblement' for trustin';
For sticks were up, and stones they flew,
Their gentle bodies bruisin',
An' in a hurry they withdrew
Fro' such unmanner'd usin'.

Then, proudly let our banner wave,
Wi' freedom's emblem o'er it,
An' toasted be the Stockport lads,
The lads who bravely bore it.
And' let the 'war-worn' Yeomanry
Go curse their sad disasters,
An' count, in rueful agony
Their bruises an' their plasters.

Samuel Bamford

Imprisoned: 1817 and 1819

In March 2011, thousands of people took to the streets of cities across Syria. Initially protesting the arrest and torture of fifteen young students who had sprayed anti-government graffiti on the walls of Daraa city in the south-west of the country, the movement developed into a wider call for democracy and demanded an end to President Bashar al-Assad's regime. They were met by a massive crackdown in which, in just one month, over 250 people were killed, and thousands arrested. **Dia'a al-Abdullah** was among the protestors. In June 2011, he was imprisoned until his release in January 2012. He remained undeterred, and was arrested a month later, in February, for posting an open letter to President al-Assad titled 'As a Syrian Citizen, I Denounce' on Facebook. Accused of insulting the president, he was tried in April 2012. What happened to him since is unknown. Al-Abdullah's poem, *The Crypt,* was written while he was in prison in 2011, where, held in solitary confinement, he suffered torture and beatings.

The Crypt

Violence is
the means of people:
The jailor kills me with a sword
I answer with a word,
and he sets my pages alight

Oh God
I burn the cigarettes of these days
in my cell
My heart is the fifth wall;
I set it alight

Eid is coming
And it will bring
Only bad tobacco to smoke,
so I leave it aside

You promised
my heart would be made only for love;
now I am so enraged
– save me,
cover my heart with tenderness
Make it strong,
Offer him a touch
… a laugh …
…
So, this is my homeland;
I became its enemy
by speaking out
Speaking out brings pain –
but how can we not?
…
My homeland,
I touch your hands
from behind bars
…

Dia'a al-Abdullah

Disappeared: 2012

Translated from Arabic by Ghias Aljundi

Anna Barkova

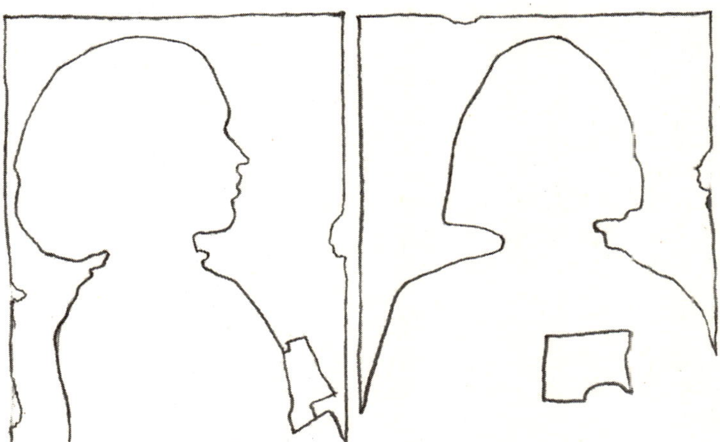

Anna Barkova was a sixteen-year-old Bolshevik youth activist at the start of the Russian Revolution in 1917. She was a member of the Circle of Genuine Proletarian Poets. Her poems brought her to the attention of the Bolshevik establishment and she got an administrative job at the Kremlin in 1922. The same year, her poetry collection, *Woman,* was published, followed in 1923 by the play *Natas'ia Bonfire* (Natas'ia Kostër). She also worked for the government newspaper *Pravda,* where her poems appeared. Becoming disillusioned with Soviet life in the 1920s, she spoke of the repression of individual freedoms. She was never able to publish again. In 1934, Barkova was arrested for comments she made in private after the murder of the Bolshevik leader Sergei Kirov; she suggested that 'the wrong man had been killed'. She was sentenced to five years in prison and sent into internal exile. She was again imprisoned from 1947 to 1955. She was sentenced a third time in 1957, and released, and again sent into two years' exile, in 1965. In all the trials, her notebooks and poems, including *I Want to Stay Calm,* were used as evidence of dissent. She spent the rest of her life in poverty. Her writings, including hundreds written in prison, lay undiscovered until the fall of the Soviet Union.

I Want to Stay Calm

I want to stay calm,
To look at everything dispassionately.
I'm surely not going to dash,
Mindlessly, like everyone else, ahead?

We try to distract ourselves with construction projects,
To burn with enthusiasm, raise banners,
Although everyone dreams of lying down
To doze in their own bed.

It can't be helped. We are tired.
People are just people.
Enough blood has been given to strengthen
the sick, historic age.

It betrayed our hopes,
It mocked our love,
It promised us victories
And gave us new despots.

We were naïve. We dreamed
Of leading humanity into paradise.
Dreamed of finding sacred tablets
Once we had climbed up a new Mount Sinai.

But it all turned out to be an illusion,
As it always was and will be.
And people will become corrupt and drunken,
And cynically wicked.

But later they will return to morals,
They will be moderate and strict.
Alas, we will not be the ones to make
The leap into the kingdom of freedom.

Anna Barkova

Imprisoned: 1934, 1947, 1957

Translated from Russian by Katharine Hodgson

Sedigeh Vasmaghi

Sedigeh Vasmaghi is an Iranian academic acclaimed for her work on Islamic jurisprudence. Her books are banned in Iran but published abroad. Her work is respected for insights into such issues as polygamy, women's rights and family rights. Vasmaghi is also a poet, with five published poetry collections. She also translates classical Arab poetry into Persian. Vasmaghi is an outspoken defender of human rights in Iran, which has earned her years of harassment, arrest and court cases. In August 2020, she was sentenced to six years in prison for her advocacy for human rights, including signing a petition protesting the abuses and killings of pro-democracy protestors in 2019. In 2011, she fled Iran on hearing that she was about to be arrested. She spent six years holding academic and literary posts in Europe before returning to Iran in 2017. She was promptly detained at the airport there. Although she has been convicted and there is no longer a chance of appeal, Vasmaghi has yet to be taken to prison, a frequent practice in Iran, where political activists can wait, sometimes for years, for the knock on the door summoning them to jail.

Our Bread

See there,
On the street a woman exchanges
her body for bread
and a man close by
robs another
of the bread he is carrying home
And we who hang around hungrily
know that a dirty hand
has emptied our table of bread

This is our bread money turned
into yellowcake in hidden corridors
to decorate the table of oppression

The bread money has been turned into missiles
that reach Israel
faster than water and fodder
to the earthquake victims
in Varzaghan and Ahar

See these
Shells and tank skeletons
scattered over the streets of Homs
They are our bread money

See that is our bread money
Buried under the ruins of Damascus
Next to a gambler's hopes

Look, this is our bread money
Spent on the streets of Aleppo
In the sight of the dead
Given to a loser who has lost the game
before it has begun

...

Sedigeh Vasmaghi

Imprisoned: 1997 to date

Translated from Persian by Milena Rampoldi

Allen Ginsberg was the most significant figure of the 'Beat' generation and of the counterculture of the 1960s in the US. His most influential work is the epic poem *Howl* denouncing the destruction of the 'finest minds of my generation' through capitalist exploitation and subjugation. In 1957, its publisher, Lawrence Ferlinghetti, was tried for 'obscenity' for its explicit references to sex, both homosexual and heterosexual, and drug use. However, the judge overturned the charge, seeing the poem as of 'redeeming social importance'. It took rather longer for a court in Italy to come to a similar conclusion when, in 1967, Ginsberg was briefly arrested after reading his poem *Who Be Kind To* at a literary festival in Spoleto. Legal hearings into whether 'certain words' were obscene went on for five years before the charges were finally dismissed. Ginsberg regularly had brushes with the law, starting when he was at university. Arrested with a group of friends who were transporting stolen goods, he was given the option of jail or mental hospital and chose the latter. Widely travelled, he was arrested in several countries because of his lifestyle. A peace activist, he took part in anti-war demonstrations in the US, and was arrested on at least three occasions.

Who Be Kind To

...
Be kind to the universe of Self that
trembles and shudders and thrills
in XX Century,
that opens its eyes and belly and breast
chained with flesh to feel
the myriad flowers of bliss
that I Am to Thee–
A dream! A Dream! I don't want to be alone!
I want to know that I am loved!

I want the orgy of our flesh, orgy
of all eyes happy, orgy of the soul
kissing and blessing its mortal-grown
body, orgy of tenderness beneath the neck, orgy of
kindness to thigh and vagina
Desire given with meat hand
and cock, desire taken with
mouth and ass, desire returned
to the last sigh!
Tonite let's all make love in London
as if it were 2001 the years
of thrilling god–
And be kind to the poor soul that cries in
a crack of the pavement because he
has no body–
Prayers to the ghosts and demons, the
lackloves of Capitals & Congresses
who make sadistic noises
on the radio–
Statue destroyers & tank captains, unhappy
murderers in Mekong & Stanleyville,
That a new kind of man has come to his bliss
to end the cold war he has borne

against his own kind flesh
since the days of the snake.

Allen Ginsberg

Arrested: various occassions 1949–1967

Wole Soyinka

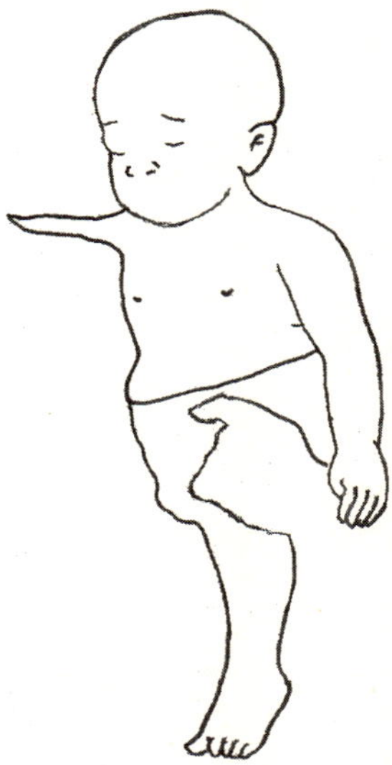

Novelist, poet and playwright **Wole Soyinka** has played an active role in Nigerian politics, for which he has been attacked, imprisoned and exiled over the decades. In the 1960s, Soyinka taught literature in Nigerian universities and founded a theatrical company that produced plays that mocked authority figures. He has long championed Nigerian democracy, notably during the 1967–1970 Biafran civil war, when up to two million Biafrans died of starvation. He attempted peace missions but was instead arrested and imprisoned for nearly two years between 1967 and 1969, spending much of the time in solitary confinement. He was never charged or tried. He wrote of this experience in papers smuggled out of jail and these were published in 1972. Soyinka spent periods in exile through the 1970s to the 1990s, including between 1994 and 1998, when he was sentenced to death in absentia for campaigning for sanctions against Nigeria over its acute human rights abuses. Soyinka has published a large body of work that criticises the abuse of power, and he was the first writer from Africa to be awarded the Nobel Prize for Literature, in 1986. After many years living in the US, Soyinka now lives in South Africa, where he moved in protest against the 2016 election of Donald Trump as president.

Civilian and Soldier

My apparition rose from the fall of lead,
Declared, 'I am a civilian.' It only served
To aggravate your fright. For how could I
Have risen, a being of this world, in that hour
Of impartial death! And I thought also: nor is
Your quarrel of this world.

You stood still
For both eternities, and oh I heard the lesson
Of your traing sessions, cautioning –
Scorch earth behind you, do not leave
A dubious neutral to the rear. Reiteration
Of my civilian quandary, burrowing earth
From the lead festival of your more eager friends
Worked the worse on your confusion, and when
You brought the gun to bear on me, and death
Twitched me gently in the eye, your plight
And all of you came clear to me.

I hope some day
Intent upon my trade of living, to be checked
In stride by your apparition in a trench,
Signalling, I am a soldier. No hesitation then
But I shall shoot you clean and fair
With meat and bread, a gourd of wine
A bunch of breasts from either arm, and that
Lone question – do you friend, even now, know
What it is all about?

Wole Soyinka

Imprisoned: 1967–1969

Majrooh Sultanpuri was one of the best-known lyricists in the Hindi film industry. He was also a highly acclaimed Urdu poet and activist. He was imprisoned in the late 1940s for reciting one of his poems. After India gained independence in 1947, there was an unsettled period during which a new constitution was drawn up, aimed at creating a republic with universal franchise, respecting all communities and addressing social deprivations and class injustices. Protests and demonstrations demanding full democratic rights were rife. A member of the leftist Progressive Writers' Association, Khan, who had adopted the pen name Majrooh (meaning 'wounded'), recited a poem at one such rally, denouncing Prime Minister Jawaharlal Nehru. Using strong language, he portrayed Nehru as a 'slave of the Commonwealth' and 'a Hitler'. Asked to apologise, Majrooh refused and as a result was sentenced to two years in prison. Majrooh's political leanings did not hinder his success as a film songwriter. He wrote hundreds of songs for Hindi film soundtracks, many of which became popular classics. He was also known for his progressive Urdu ghazals.

Slave of the Commonwealth, Nehru

Carrying the poison of dollars in its heart
roams non-violence in India

No, they cannot disguise themselves
wearing the snakeskin of khadi

Who says the flag of peace
cannot be unfurled over this land?

He looks like follower of Hitler
Punch him, friends, don't let him escape

Nehru is a slave of the Commonwealth
Strike him, friends, don't let him escape!

...

Majrooh Sultanpuri

Imprisoned: 1951

Translated from Urdu by Gopika Jadeja

'Back then, I did not understand why my mother gave me the cold shoulder. After becoming a parent of two boys, I began to understand her.'

Kim Young-joo, who came to live under under surveillance, after falling in love and marrying dissident poet.
Kim Chi-ha

Kim Chi-ha, one of South Korea's most noted popular dissident poets, was imprisoned for his writings on several occasions under anti-communist laws during the turbulent 1970s. Active in the anti-government student movement, Kim was first imprisoned in 1964–1965. He was then held in a tuberculosis sanatorium for two years, where he wrote his best-known poem *Five Bandits,* a scathing satire portraying the political, military and business elite as corrupt and decadent. When it was published in 1970, he was arrested again, and then released on bail. In March 1972, he was arrested once more, this time for his poem *Groundless Rumours,* and returned to the sanatorium for three months. In 1974, Kim wrote *Cry of the People,* an angry denunciation of emergency measures. It was secretly printed and distributed by hand. For this, he was again arrested and sentenced to death, which was then commuted to life imprisonment. He was released in 1975, only to be rearrested when he gave interviews to the press about his time in prison, including the torture to which he was subjected. He was released in 1980, after which he has continued to write. In 2013, Kim was formally acquitted on the charges of violating anti-communism laws, under which he was first imprisoned in 1974.

Five Bandits

…

Oh, here's the den of the Five Bandits, by name ConglomerApe, AssemblyMutt, TopCivilSerpent, General-in-Chimp and HighMinisCur,* all ferocious under heaven,
guts swollen big as Namsan hill, throats as tough as Dong Zhuo's navel.
Ordinary folk all have five viscera and six organs in their bellies,
but these thugs have an additional thieving gland, as big as an ox's balls, inside their bellies, so they have five viscera and seven organs,
and though originally they all learned thieving from one boss, now they each have their specialty.
As they engage in thieving day and night, their skills are god-given, pretty well.

One day the five thugs met together and said:
It's ten years since we went into the thievery business, sealing an oath in blood,
day in day out, we've piled up mountains of know-how and gold, so what about staking a hundred thousand pounds of gold
and holding a contest to show off the feats we've perfected in all these years?

…

The first comes forward, ConglomerApe's his name.
Wearing clothes made of money, the hat on his head made of money, the shoes on his feet made of money, the gloves on his hands made of money,
gold watch, gold ring, gold bangle, gold buttons, gold tie-pin, gold cuff-links, gold buckles, gold teeth, gold finger-nails, gold toe-nails, gold zippers, gold watch-strap, he comes forward.
His big ass drooping, his great belly bulging, poop-poop farting, he comes slithering forward.

…

Another comes forward.
AssemblyMutt comes forward.
Back bent like a hunchback, slit-eyed like Cao Cao,
he comes forward lisping in a wheezing voice.

…

* The 'Five Bandits' is a term often applied by Koreans to five high Korean officials who supported the Japanese annexation of Korea in 1910, so betraying the country. The poet used special Chinese characters for the names of the Bandits. Pronounced in Korean fashion, they sound like the words 'Conglomerate, Assemblyman, High Civil Servant, General and Minister' – 재벌(狾□), 국회의원(?獪狋猿), 고급공무원(跍□功無猿), 장성(長猩), 장차관(暲차 犭+ 差矔) – but several of the Chinese characters use the radical 'dog' or are otherwise related to dogs, pigs, monkeys, etc., to suggest the bestial quality of these figures in an insulting way. This cannot be paralleled in English, of course, and a parodic parallel has been invented using ConglomerApe, AssemblyMutt, TopCivilSerpent, General-in-Chimp and HighMinisCur.

The third comes forward. TopCivilSerpent comes forward.
His body shaped like a rubber balloon, eyes like those of a venomous snake, corpselike,blue, rigid flesh,
with tightly clenched lips, he's obviously a cleanhanded official.

...

The fourth comes forward. General-in-Chimp's his name.
In height he's tall as an eight-foot-high wall,
the line of low-ranking soldiers under his command is as long as the Great Wall,
with hairs sticking out all over his body, white rings round the irises of his eyes, a tiger's jaws, twitching nose, a short bristly beard, quite obviously an animal.

...

The last one comes forward.
HighMinisCur comes forward.
His tongue coated white, full of dregs of wine sticking out all over, he emerges, glaring eyes veiled by disgusting mucus, his left hand conducts the national defensewith a golf-club.

...

Next, the Five Bandits summon the police chief and, condescending to acknowledge his laudable valor,
invite him to be their guard, living in the kennel beside the main gate of their mansion.
On hearing that, the police chief is thrilled with delight.
He shouts for joy, tra la la. He brings along all kinds of weapons, arranges them in solemn order, lives happily ever after in his kennel,
until one bright, cloudless morning, suddenly, just as he was stretching, struck by lightning, he died.
Just then, the story goes, the Five Bandits dropped dead too, blood spouting from every one of their six orifices. Ha ha ha.
All their deeds, unforgotten, have remained alive in the mouths of a hundred generations,
passed down at length until at last they found fertile soil in a poor beggar poet like myself.

Kim Chi-ha

Imprisoned: Several occasions 1964–1980

Translated from Korean by Brother Antony

Abdellatif Laâbi is one of Morocco's most acclaimed present-day poets, known for his politically engaged writing. He spent several years in jail in the 1970s for 'crimes of opinion'. In 1966, Laâbi had founded the literary magazine *Souffle* with other like-minded writers. It showcased new, young, avant-garde Moroccan writers. Left-leaning, it was at the heart of the revolutionary spirit that swept across North Africa in the 1960s. Laâbi was also a member of the Moroccan Communist Party, and set up the political group known as 'Forward'. In January 1972, during the harsh rule of King Hassan II, Laâbi was arrested, and the following year, *Souffle* was forced to shut down. Laâbi was sentenced to ten years' imprisonment in 1973 for 'conspiracy against the state' and 'crimes of opinion'. He served eight and a half years in prison, during which, as he described it in his prison writings, he suffered appalling conditions, including torture. He was released in 1980 under an amnesty programme and, in 1985, he left Morocco for France, where he lives to this day. He has published seventeen collections of poetry, novels and other forms of writing since.

Glory to Those Who Torture Us

from you to me
                    the truth
swear you won't believe me
we are waiting
for a wheel to break open inedible flesh
or for an eye to be extinguished for having witnessed
no predator will come stitch up the C-sections
we torture
            glorify
artifice of pogroms
                            bonfire of skeletons

glory   glory
we are the chosen people
erected
          upon the peaks of fate
for us the tomorrows that sing
rivers of honey
                          and milk
sacrifice brothers
                        sacrifice
exile in sacrifice
o the apotheosis of throats ready
                                    for the sacrifice
heritage
            Abraham's sadism
heritage
            faith struck down by miracles
the desert's spontaneous abundance
m i r a c l e
                  we do not suffer
o the hired killer's unblemished brow
the tickling of electrodes
and the scalpel stripping the vertebrae
again
        and again
breathing in all the gases
                              greedily
                                      swallowing the grenades

glory
to the firing squad
embracing the wrong side
                                and the right side

of the ripe finger
        that fondles
               the trigger
                     that kills us
the cast iron sparkles
stillborn
skirted the scalping
          of the pecking order
I didn't want to partake in this spectacle
no
puppet
   I didn't want them to execute me
ludicrously
      on the bleachers
but to remain a valve
            seaweed

a body throbbing with elemental breath
diastole
   to remain a pharynx
                without
a shot at the strongest life
to be of this night
            that doesn't dismantle the day
of this leavening
          not of this dough
to be at last of these poisonous knots of roots

a blanket refusal
this so-called complication of speaking organisms
I refuse
     this procreating of automatons
you've have drawn blood from the language
and the world

...

Abdellatif Laâbi

Imprisoned: 1972–1980

Translated from French by André Naffis-Sahely

Regino Pedroso was born in 1896 in Matanzas, Cuba, then a sugar plantation region. He worked in the sugar fields before moving to Havana as an artisan and mechanic. He went on to publish several collections of poetry on the themes of racial injustice and radical politics. One such example is *Black Brother* (Hermano Negro), published in 1939, an excoriating call for political mobilisation to end discrimination against Afro-Cubans. Pedroso was awarded the 1939 Cuba National Poetry Award for his collection *Beyond the Sea Sings* (Màs allá cantra el mar) even though it included poems for which he had been imprisoned in 1935 for six months on charges of 'seditious propaganda'. Heavily involved in radical politics, Pedroso had been editor of *The Word* (La Palabra), the first newspaper of the then banned Cuban Communist Party. When the Communist Party was legalised in 1938, Pedroso's work could be published, even works for which he had earlier been imprisoned. His 1955 collection *The Plum Tree of Yuan Pei Fu* (El Ciruelo de Yuan Pei Fu) explored his Chinese heritage.

Brother Negro

Negro, brother negro,
you are in me: speak!
Negro, brother negro,
I am in you: Sing!
Your voice lies in my voice,
your anguish in my voice,
your blood in my voice ...
I, too, am your race!

You are able to sing,
because the jungle gave you its nights of ferocious rhythms;
you are able to weep,
because the great rivers gave you a torrent of tears.

For his enjoyment
the rich man makes a game of you.
And in Paris, New York, Madrid, and Havana,
like figurines
they make straw negroes for export;
there are men who fulfill your starvation with laughter:
they traffic with your sweat,
the trade with your pain,
and you laugh, you surrender, and you dance.

Negro, brother negro,
silence your maracas just a bit.
And learn here,
and look there.
And listen there in Scottsboro, in Scottsboro,
among the cries of slave anguish
man's yearnings,
man's rage,
human pain and desire for a man without a race.

Negro, brother negro,
muffle your bongo just a tad.

Are we not more than black?
Are we not more than merry?
Are we not more than rumba, black lechery and comparsas?
Are we not more than grins and color,
grins and color?

Learn here,
and listen there,
and look there in Scottsboro, in Scottsboro,
dressed in Negro skin,
men that bleed.

Negro, brother negro;
more brotherly in desire than in race
Negro in Haiti, Negro in Jamaika, Negro in New York,
Negro in Havana – pain that sells
exploitation in shop windows –
listen there in Scottsboro, in Scottsboro, in Scottsboro …
Give the world with your rebellious anguish
your human voice …
and for a moment silence your maracas!

Regino Pedroso

Imprisoned: 1935

Translated from Spanish by John A. Gronbeck-Tedesco

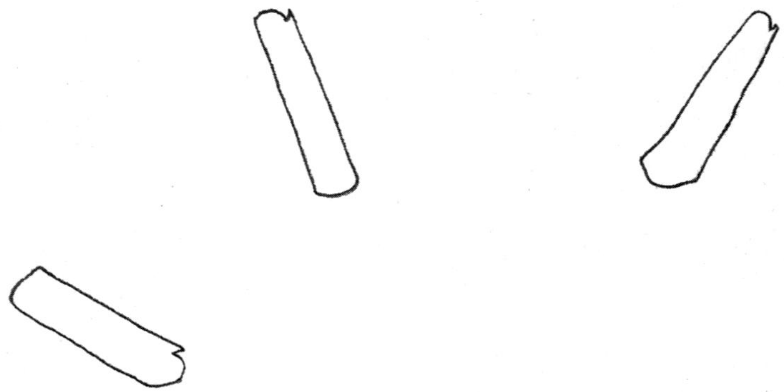

Scratched on soap, memorised, washed away.
Then written on cigarette papers, smuggled
outside the prison.

Irina Ratushinskaya

Irina Ratushinskaya was imprisoned for three years in a women's penal colony in the Soviet Gulag. During that time, she wrote, and her writings are searing accounts of the acute hardships the prisoners endured. Yet, they also speak of the camaraderie between the prisoners, and the humanity they shared in those harsh conditions. Ratushinskaya was first arrested in 1981. She was arrested again in 1982 for five of her samizdat poems. Ratushinskaya was a staunch Christian during the time of Soviet anti-religious persecution. Her poetry reflected her religious faith. She never wrote on politics, saying that the subject was too 'low' for verse. Yet, she was convicted of anti-Soviet propaganda and sentenced to seven years in prison, followed by five years' internal exile, a sentence that was internationally condemned. In the Gulag, Ratushinskaya continued to write poetry. Denied pen and paper, she wrote with matchsticks on slivers of soap, memorising the verses before washing them away. She was released into exile in 1986 on the eve of a summit between presidents Ronald Reagan of the US and Mikhail Gorbachev of the USSR. Ratushinskaya and her family lived in exile in Britain until she regained her Russian citizenship and they returned in 1998.

A Letter to 1921

for Nikolai Gumilev

Leave on this side of the earth
Post-mortem trial and the unjust sentence.
You've been hundredfold entwined by
Your cruel motherland's grassroots.
From the land that ceased to be,
That struggled all alone with itself,
From the whirlpool of Russian riots and revolts—
I hear your calm voice.
The midnight hour hits me in the temple.
Yes, conquistador! Yes, a stubborn architect!
Your Russia has no more verse lines left.
It has the tongue of leaden dots of ellipsis instead.
You sure know it, don't you? So
Do instruct me
In my despair at the last barricade,
When they croak:
Fire! Fire!—

To understand and to forgive—but not to beg for mercy!
And let the grass whirl in a mournful ritual—
It won't be strained—it used to it.
But maybe I will find the right words then
With which I will appear before God.

Irina Ratushinskaya

Imprisoned: 1981, 1982–1986

Translated from Russian by Ian Probstein

Giordano Bruno

Giordano Bruno was a philosopher, astronomer, mathematician and poet. He was executed at the stake as a heretic under the Catholic Inquisition in Italy. Bruno explored scientific and theological ideas that brought him at odds with the religious leadership of the time. A follower of Copernicus, he wrote about his theory that the universe is infinite, and challenged religious doctrines. Bruno was a Dominican friar for twelve years. He abandoned the order and left Italy in 1576 to avoid the Inquisition. For the next fifteen years, he led a peripatetic life in France, England, Germany and Prague under influential patrons, including Henry III, who admired him for his astonishing memory and teachings on mnemonics. He published numerous books and poems, yet, everywhere he went, he caused controversy, leaving under a cloud. In 1591, Bruno returned to Italy believing that the Inquisition had relaxed. He was arrested and tried for opinions contrary to the Catholic faith. Throughout the seven-year trial, he refused to recant, saying that his views were not incompatible with Christian concepts. On 17 February 1600, he was burned at the stake in a public square in Rome. In 2000, the Vatican called his death a 'sad episode' but said that the church at that time was justified in condemning him.

On the Infinite, the Universe and the Worlds

My solitary passage to those parts,
Born of my thoughts, rising to the courts of infinity,
I would gather every skill of arts and sciences,
Be reborn there, there raise for you

…

Escaped from the black and confining prison,
That held me so tightly for many years,
Freed from the chains that constricted me,
And the person who has been my enemy,
Who kept me in night's darkness,
He can no longer threaten me,
For I have faced the great Python,
The Fury's blood rejoins the sea,
I give thanks to you, my sweet voice,
I thank you, my sun, my divine light,
I dedicate to you my heart, moreover my hands,
You have led me to an exalted place,
Your attentions have healed me.

Who makes me soar, who warms my heart,
So I no longer fear misfortune or death?
Who broke those chains and those doors?
Who hid me in the forest?
The ages, the years, the months, the days, the hours,
Those daughters of time, armed with his weapons,
Made of iron, of diamond, of power,
Have assured me of his might,
Yet I affix these wings, leap in the air,
And surge into the skies, 'til in the infinite I stand,
Leaving my globe behind to join the others,
And as I travel farther in the infinite field,
I leave what others have seen far behind me.

Giordano Bruno

Executed: 1600

Translated from Italian by Scott Gosnell

Rabi'a Balkhi was a poet-princess of the noble court of Balkh in northern Afghanistan. The first woman poet in the history of Persian poetry, Balkhi's poems were admired by the leading intellectuals of the day. It was her secret love for a Turkic slave, Bhaktas, owned by her brother, the emir Haris, that led to the tragedy of her death. She wrote poems to Bhaktas that told of her love for him. When Haris discovered these, he was driven into a rage, imprisoned Balkhi in a hammam (a bath), and threw Bhaktas into a well. In despair, Balkhi slashed her wrists, writing her last poems to Bhaktas in her blood on the walls as she died. Bhaktas survived, and on finding Balkhi dead, murdered Haris and then committed suicide. Balkhi's tragic story has been retold through the centuries, with different emphases, depending on the time and place. She is a feminist icon to some, to others a victim of honour in a patriarchal society, and to others a martyr to sacred love. Still an important cultural figure today, she features in Afghan film, theatre and art. Public institutions, women's schools and hospitals bear her name.

Love's Web

I am captured by your love
trying to escape is not possible
love is an ocean without boundaries
a wise person would not want to swim in it
if you want love until the end
you must accept what is not accepted
welcome hardship with joy
eat poison but call it honey

Rabi'a Balkhi

Died: Tenth century (cause unknown, execution or suicide)

Translated from Persian by Bashir Sakhwaraz

Saw Wai

Saw Wai is a Burmese political activist who was imprisoned for his playful love poem which contained a hidden message ridiculing the Burmese leader Than Shwe. In February 2008, an eight-line poem appeared in the Yangon magazine *The Love Journal*. It was titled *February 14*. On the surface it was a love poem celebrating Valentine's Day, in which a broken-hearted man who has been rejected by a fashion model thanks her for teaching him the meaning of love. However, the poem is an acrostic, where the first letters of each sentence when read downwards reveal a hidden message. Saw Wai's was: *General Than Shwe is Crazy with Power*. He was arrested, charged with 'harming public tranquillity' and imprisoned for more than two years. Saw Wai has a history of activism. He was sacked from his job in 1988 for his involvement in the democracy movement. In October 2019, he was again arrested, this time for a speech calling for democratic reform, during which he encouraged the audience to chant the refrain from a poem: 'reject evil laws'. He was bailed on health grounds in February 2020 and his trial is delayed due to the COVID-19 pandemic.

February 14

Ehrenburg said
Only if you know how to suffer painfully
Only if you are crazy-crazy
Can you appreciate a great work of Art
Dear little photo model who makes me dizzy
They say it is a broken liver disease,
Millions of those who know how to love
Laugh and clap those gold-gilded hands.

[Translator's note: 'Broken heart' in Burmese is usually expressed as a broken liver]

Saw Wai

Imprisoned: 2008–2010; On trial: 2019

Translated from Burmese

Just as the 1968 revolution roiled across Europe, Mexico and North America, demonstrators in Turkey also revolted against the establishment, staging street protests and university occupations. As elsewhere, these were met with police brutality, arrests and imprisonment. The figure of Che Guevara was iconic for these revolutionary movements as a symbol of the struggle against imperialism. Che inspired **Metin Demirtaş** to write a poem dedicated to him. For this poem, he was arrested in June 1968, at a time when Turkey was keen to be aligned with the anti-communist West. Demirtaş was acquitted and released just one month later, after his defence lawyer pointed out that although Che was a communist, he was also an anti-imperialist and as such his cause could be compared with the Turkish nationalist struggle against the Ottoman Empire. Demirtaş continued to get into trouble with the authorities, such as in 1988, when he was once again briefly arrested for his writings.

Che Guevara

Che Guevara, we too have our mountains
Don't worry if they are still now, still like falcons,
They are weary, have seen wars, hosted partisans,
Yet, they are not traitors, if no rifle is fired,
Their guns lean against the pines and oaks
We too have our mountains Che Guevara.

Che Guevara, we too have our people here
Forsaken in the warm winds of distant fields
Committed to brotherhood with ballads
Like all the people of the world
And moving only in storms and thunder
We too have our people here Che Guevara.

Che Guevara, we too have our poets
They too have survived rooms of stone, rooms of no sun
Their hearts beating for peace and love
One half is steel anger, while the other is docile blue
They too have passed through iron gates upright
We too have our beautiful people Che Guevara.

Che Guevara, we too have our young men
Who have made their way out of poverty here
By feeding on only a few olives and bread at universities
Young men hit by girls like sirens, then by alcohol
Wandering alone the streets in anger
And who rebel when they realize the truth.

For Vietnam is our Vietnam
Congo is our Congo
Once the sap runs in the branches
Darkness blows up with pains in deep
To reach that beautiful tomorrow
Che Guevara, we too have our mountains.

Metin Demirtaş

Imprisoned: 1968

Translated from Turkish by Yusuf Eradam

Malay Roychoudhury was born in Bihar, India, in 1939. He came to international fame in 1964, when he and ten others were brought to trial on charges of obscenity and subversion. They were members of the Hungryalists, a movement founded by Roychoudhury and others in 1961, which challenged the rigid narrative forms of pre-existing colonial perspectives in Bengali literature. Beat poets Allen Ginsberg and Laurence Ferlinghetti admired their subversive defiance of traditional literature, in ways that were similar to the Beat Generation movement. Central to the trial was Roychoudhury's poem *Stark Electric Jesus* (Prachanda Boidytik Chhutar), published in 1964, and accused of obscenity and blasphemy. The cases against all but Roychoudhury (the leader of the movement), were dropped. Despite an international campaign calling for an end to the trial, it dragged on for almost three years until, in 1967, Roychoudhury was found guilty and sentenced to a month in prison. This was later commuted to a fine equivalent to two months' salary. The lengthy and convoluted hearings were aimed to deter anyone who dared consider challenging the establishment. Roychoudhury lives in Mumbai, where he continues to write poems, novels and essays.

Stark Electric Jesus

Oh I'll die I'll die I'll die
My skin is in blazing furore
I do not know what I'll do where I'll go oh I am sick
I'll kick all Arts in the back and go away Shubha
Shubha let me go and live in your cloaked melon
In the unfastened shadow of dark destroyed saffron curtain
The last anchor is leaving me after I got the other anchors lifted
I can't resist anymore, a million glasspanes are breaking in my cortex
I know, Shubha, spread out your matrix, give me peace
Each vein is carrying a stream of tears up to the heart
Brain's contagious flints are decomposing out of eternal sickness
Mother why didn't you give me birth in the form of a skeleton
I'd have gone two billion light-years and kissed God's arse
But nothing pleases me nothing sounds well
I feel nauseated with more than a single kiss
I've forgotten women during copulation and returned to the Muse
I do not know what these happenings are but they are occurring within me
I'll destroy and shatter everything
Draw and elevate Shubha into my hunger
Shubha will have to be given
Oh Malay
Kolkata seems to be a procession of wet and slippery organs today
But I do not know what I'll do now with my own self
My power of recollection is withering away
Let me ascend alone toward death
I haven't had to learn copulation and dying
I haven't had to learn the responsibility of shedding the last drops after urination
Haven't had to learn to go and lie beside Shubha in the darkness
Have not had to learn the usage of French leather while lying on Nandita's bosom
Though I wanted the healthy spirit of Aleya's fresh chinarose matrix
Yet I submitted to the refuge of my brain's cataclysm
I am failing to understand why I still want to live

...

Malay Roychoudhury

On trial: 1964–1967

Translated from Bengali by Malay Roychoudhury

Ericson Acosta is a student activist, journalist and poet. He spent two years in prison on charges that were later dismissed as groundless. Ericson was arrested by the military in February 2011 in San Jorge, Samar, a beautiful spot in central Philippines, on suspicion of being a member of the New People's Army, a communist guerrilla group, and possessing explosives. Although he was kept in a civilian prison, he was held under the watch of army officers. He suffered from kidney problems, but was denied adequate medical care during his imprisonment. Yet, he continued to write. Supporters said the arrest was without any foundation and rallied round his cause. The Free Ericson Acosta campaign was launched, arguing that he was being arrested for his human rights advocacy and being part of student protests. Arts and rights organisations in the Philippines and abroad called for his release. In January 2013, the Philippines Department of Justice agreed to Acosta's petition to review the criminal case. It found that there had been 'numerous irregularities' in his arrest and detention, which raised serious doubts concerning 'the validity of the charges against him'. He was released a month later and returned to writing and publishing poetry, and political activism.

And So Your Poetry Must

Be wary you say
of its claims
lest you waive art
to us millions unworthy
of taste and manner
lest you be christened
peddler of images
alien in form
pagan in content
lest your license
be forfeited

...

And so while you summon
the litany of worlds
your own words fashion
you annul my existence
and those of millions
whose narratives you say
betray poetic tone
make burlesque of beauty
and thus like scarecrows
set even the most heretic
muses scurrying back
to their sanctum of rules.

...

And so with your eulogies
to passion
to rage against time
to pledge with life's gift
you lull the birth
of noise
of revenge
of bloodshow
that shall feed millions
complete history
and perhaps spare poetry.

Ericson Acosta

Imprisoned: 2011–2013

Roque Antonio García, known by his pen name, **Roque Dalton**, was a poet with near mythical status for his notoriously bohemian lifestyle and his role in El Salvador's revolutionary movement. He was executed in 1975, just before his fortieth birthday, by the forces to which he was loyal and had represented. In 1973, Dalton had joined the People's Revolutionary Party (ERP), a leftist guerrilla movement. By then, he had already spent three stints in prison for sedition for his activities as a communist, once famously escaping when his prison walls collapsed during an earthquake. He spent much of the 1960s either in prison or in exile in Mexico, Czechoslovakia and Cuba. But he soon fell out with the ERP. Accusing him of insubordination and of being a Central Intelligence Agency (CIA) spy, its leadership ordered his execution, and he was shot dead in May 1975. His remains have never been found. Alongside his political activity, Dalton was a prolific poet. During his lifetime, he published eighteen collections of poetry, novels and essays. These were often humorous and dealt with life, death, love and politics. His work was prohibited for years, but Dalton's execution is now officially acknowledged by the El Salvador authorities as a 'terrible mistake', and he has been given status as the country's greatest poet. His family continues to call for justice, as two people involved in his murder now hold leading government positions.

Bad News on a Scrap of Newspaper

These days when my friends die
only their names die.

How can one yearn from the inhuman pit
to grasp more than newsprint,
shiny black wispy letters,
arrows sunk into private memories?

Only one who lives outside prison walls
can honor the corpses, cleanse himself
of sorrow for his dead with embraces,
clutch gravestones with fingernails and tears.

Not so the prisoners: we just whistle
so the echo drowns out the news.

Roque Dalton

Imprisoned 1959 onwards; exiled 1960s; executed 1975

Translated from Spanish by Kelly Washbourne

Though under house arrest, his poem was put to music and circulated on cassettes.

Hadraawi

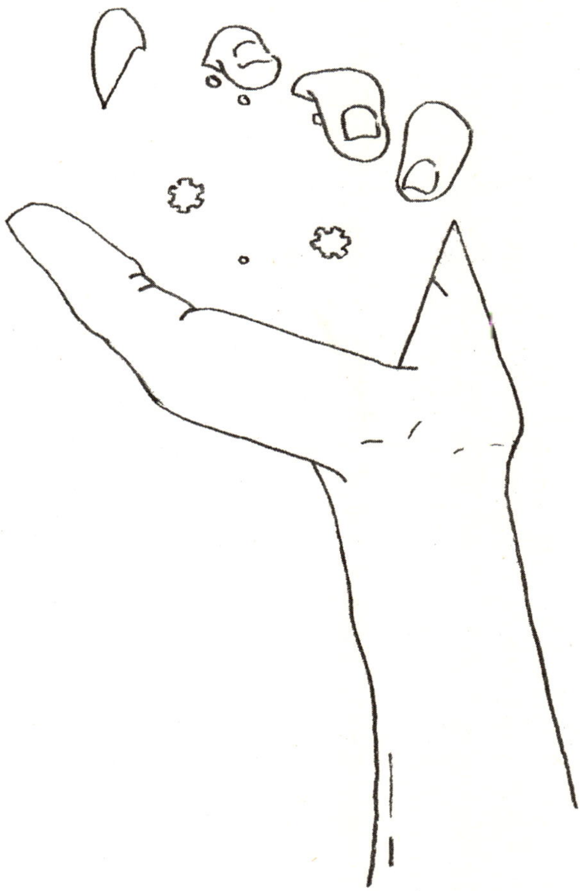

Mohamad Ibrahim Warsame Hadraawi is a widely translated poet from Somaliland. His poetry focusses on social tensions, politics, love and peace. He has played a leading role in promoting peace and human rights, and has campaigned for independence for Somaliland. Born in 1943 into a nomadic camel-herding family in the then British protectorate of Somaliland, he spent his early years in Yemen before returning to Somalia after independence. It was in the 1970s that Hadraawi became known for his poetry and plays, many of which were critical of the military regime of Siad Barre. Among them is *She-Camel*, which tells of a slaughter for a feast that was enjoyed only by an elite few and watched by a multitude, a critique of the corruption under Barre's dictatorship. Hadraawi spent five years in prison between 1973 and 1978 for his writings. In 1982, he left for Ethiopia to become a leading member of the opposition Somali National Movement. He relocated to Britain in 1991, from where he performed his lyrical poems and songs across Europe and North America. He returned to Somalia in 1999 and now lives in the Somaliland capital, Hargeisa, where he teaches literature.

The Killing of the She-Camel

How they came rushing to that place
where the carcass of the she-camel lay,
and what a commotion there was
as each caught at her flesh
pair by pair clawed off their share
frying it in the glare of the sun
and cramming down dry
its crisp skin, crunching the bones.
You'd bare your teeth too to see
their scattered followers come
still cramped with greed, ravenous
at seeing the smoke ascend
from the colossal mountain's top,
scrambling up cliffs and ravines.

The snake sneaks in the castle:
although it's carpeted with thorns
still the coward casts off his curses
so the courageous must stretch out his neck;
the cob stallion sells his values
in order to cut a fine figure.
When such cockiness struts forth
and even laughter becomes a crime
our country has unfinished business.

...

Mohamad Ibrahim Warsame Hadraawi

Imprisoned: 1973–1978

Translated from Somali by W. N. Herbert, Said Jamal Hussein and Maxamed Xasan 'Alto'

Kazi Nazrul Islam, known as the Bangladesh National Poet, was born in 1899 into a Bengali Muslim family during British colonial rule. He joined the British Army during the First World War, after which he went to Kolkata, then known as Calcutta, to work as a journalist and to write. He wrote nearly 4,000 songs and poems on the themes of humanity, love and revolution. They became widely read and a source of inspiration for the Indian independence movement in which Nazrul played a part. The colonial authorities arrested Nazrul on several occasions and his books were banned. In November 1922, he was sentenced to a year in prison for sedition, for his poem *Coming of Anondomoyee* (Anondomoyeer Agomone), published in the literary magazine *Comet* (Dhumketu) that he had established in September that year. The poem invokes the Hindu warrior goddess Durga to fight against colonial rule. Nazrul's writing career was tragically cut short when he was in his forties because of a rare form of dementia that took away his powers of speech and memory, just at the time when India became free.

Coming of Anondomoyee

How much longer will you
Stay hidden behind a clay statue?
Heaven today is subjugated by merciless tyrants.
God's children are getting whipped,
Heroic youth- hanged.
India today is a butchery-when
Will you arrive, O Destroyer?
God's soldiers are serving terms of hard labor
Exiled to desolate island.
Who will come to the battlefield,
unless you come with your sword in your hand?

Kazi Nasrul Islam

Imprisoned: 1922–1923

Translated from Bengali by Sajed Kamal

Scraps of paper with poems saved by prison guards of Alicante.

Miguel Hernández Gilabert

Born into a goat-herding family, **Miguel Hernández Gilabert** struggled against his father's opposition to his becoming a poet, and he worked on the family farm for many years. Yet, he was to become one of Spain's best-known poets of the twentieth century. Like so many other artists in Franco's regime, he was persecuted for his anti-fascism. He died of tuberculosis in a prison cell in 1942, aged just thirty-one. Despite the odds against him, many collections of Hernández's poetry were published, both during his lifetime and after his death. He earned the admiration and friendship of leading artists of the time, such as Federico Garcia Lorca and Pablo Neruda. A Republican fighter during the civil war, he became famous for his poems written from the battlefield. After the war, Hernández stayed on in Spain and continued to be an outspoken critic of fascism. Judged by Franco as an 'extremely dangerous and despicable element to all good Spaniards', Hernández was sentenced to death in 1939, a sentence later reduced to thirty years. In prison, he continued to write poems, many of them on scraps of toilet paper or in letters to his wife, with some even being saved by prison guards.

The Soldier and the Snow

December has frozen its double-edged breath
and blows it down from the icy heavens,
like a dry fire coming apart in threads,
like a huge ruin that topples on soldiers.

Snow where horses have left their hoof-marks
is a solitude of grief that gallops on.
Snow like split fingernails, or claws badly worn,
like a malice out of heaven or a final contempt.

It bites, prunes, cuts through with the heavy
slash of a bloodshot and pale marble ax.
It comes down, it falls everywhere like some ruined embrace
of canyons and wings, solitude and snow.

This violence that splits off from the core of winter,
raw hunger tired of being hungry and cold,
hangs over the naked with an eternal grudge
that is white, speechless, dark, starving, and fatal.

It wants to soften down forges, hatred, flames,
it wants to stop up the seas, to bury all loves.
It goes along throwing up huge, gauzy drifts,
hostile hunks of glass, statues that say nothing.

I want the heart made of wood in every shop
and textile factory to flood over and cover
the bodies that ignite the morning
with their looks and yells, boots and rifles.

Clothes for the corpses that are able to go naked,
able to go dressed in frost and ice,
in withered stone that fights off the cruel beaks,
the pale beak thrusts and the pale escapes.

Clothes for corpses that silently fall back
the most snowy attacks with the reddest bones.
Because these soldiers have sun-fired bones,
because they are fires with footprints and eyes.

The cold hunches forward, death loses its leaves.
I can hear the noiseless sound raining down.
Red on the white snow, life turns
the steamy snow red, sows fire in the snow.

Soldiers are so much like rock crystals
that only fire, only flame shapes them,
and they fight with icy cheekbones, with their mouths,
and turn whatever they attack into memories of ash.

Miguel Hernández Gilabert

Imprisoned: 1939–1942

Maung Saung Kha

In November 2015, poet and student activist **Maung Saung Kha** had been in hiding for a month after he learned that he had been charged with defaming then Myanmar president Thein Sein in a short poem, *Portrait*. In the poem, Maung claimed to have had the image of the president tattooed on his penis. He was arrested when he was attending the trial of another activist, taken to prison, and brought to trial six months later, in May 2016. He was given a six-month sentence and released the same day for time already served. Maung said the intention of his poem was not to offend. It was a response to the practice prevalent at the time, of people getting the image of the state counsellor and leader of the pro-democracy movement, Aung San Suu Kyi, tattooed on their chests. He had asked himself, 'Where would they put a tattoo of someone they hate?' Maung also headed the Poetry Lover Association. He protested human rights abuses as the situation deteriorated in Myanmar.

Image

On my manhood rests a tattooed
portrait of Mr. President
My beloved found that out after
we wed
She was utterly gutted,
Inconsolable.

Maung Saung Kha

Imprisoned: 2015–2016

Translated from Burmese by Ko Ko Thett

In 2010, **Mohammad al-Ajami Ibn al-Dhib**, was a thirty-year-old literature student in his third year at Cairo University in Egypt. He read out a poem to a few friends at his home in Qatar. In November 2011, he was arrested in Doha, accused of 'inciting the overthrow of the ruling regime' and 'criticizing the Emir' in his poetry. Al-Ajami's trial, which led to his conviction and life imprisonment in November 2012, was riddled with flaws, including alleged tampering of evidence and secret hearings, making it difficult to be entirely clear which of the two poems cited in the trial had led to his imprisonment. One was a spoken word poem that had never been written down, which criticised Sheikh Hamad bin Khalifa al-Thani, then emir of Qatar. Someone present at the reading in Cairo had secretly recorded the performance and posted it online. The other, *Jasmine Revolution Poem,* was in praise of the Tunisian Uprising in 2011, one line of which was, 'We are all Tunisia in the face of the ruling elite.' It was accused of being a direct criticism of the emir. In February 2013, al-Ajami's sentence was reduced to fifteen years. He was pardoned and freed in March 2016.

Jasmine Revolution Poem

Prime Minister, Mohamed al-Ghannouchi:
If we measured your might
it wouldn't hold a candle
to a constitution.
We shed no tears for Ben Ali,
nor any for his reign.
It was nothing more than a moment
in time for us,
historical
and dictatorial,
a system of oppression,
an era of autocracy.
Tunisia declared the people's revolt:
When we lay blame
only the base and vile suffer from it;
and when we praise
we do so with all our hearts.
...
A warning to the country
whose people starve
while the regime boasts of its prosperity.
A warning to the country whose citizens sleep:
one moment you have your rights,
the next they're taken from you.
A warning to the system—inherited—of oppression.
How long have all of you been slaves
to one man's selfish predilections?
How long will the people remain
ignorant of their own strength,
while a despot makes decrees and appointments,
the will of the people all but forgotten?
Why is it that a ruler's decisions are carried out?
...
Why, why do these regimes
import everything from the West—
everything but the rule of law, that is,
and everything but freedom?

Mohammad al-Ajami Ibn al-Dhib

Imprisoned: 2011–2016

Translated from Arabic by Kareem James Abu-Zeid

Fatemeh Ekhtesari is an Iranian feminist poet who went into exile after being sentenced to a long prison term. She was to face lashes as part of her punishment. She is trained as a midwife. Her writings are commentaries on sexuality, gender, religion and freedom of expression. She is part of the post-modern Ghazal literary movement. Her first book, published in 2010, was banned when it was discovered that she had filled in by hand 'forbidden' words that had been blanked out by censors and had shared these copies with her friends. She also co-edited the literary magazine *It Was the Very Tomorrow* (Hamin Fard Bood), which was banned in 2008. Ekhtesari was arrested, along with poet Mehdi Mousavi, in December 2013 and spent over a month in solitary confinement before being bailed. She was sentenced in October 2015 to eleven and a half years imprisonment, plus ninety-nine lashes, for 'insulting the sacred' and indulging in propaganda. Mousavi received nine years and ninety-nine lashes. Ekhtesari was additionally charged with indecency for shaking hands with men during a literary exchange in Sweden just before her arrest. The charges could also be linked to the adaptation of her work 'A feminist discussion before boiling the potatoes' by exiled Iranian rapper Shahin Najafi. Ekhtesari and Mousavi escaped Iran in 2015 and now live in Norway.

Run

- run
A voice passed by me.
And someone just ran inside my confused mind
- run
The streets were crowded and crowded
- run
The cars were honking in an endless night
Honking after many years of forgetfulness
Entering my ear and confusing my mind
I heard them honking
And I kept a torn up picture in my hands
I heard the sound of being lost in all the dead-end streets
I heard the sound of tears slipping down the rocked eyes
I heard the sound of tear gas and cigarettes all stinging
I heard the sound of batons meeting backs and heads
And I heard the shadows running behind me
- run
Two silences made a voice
The voice of our hands separated from each other
Your voice passing by me
Your voice becoming the voice of people
And my own low voice lost in all those bad days
I was sticking to a postern
Sticking to my office to my job
Sticking to my pills in all those nights of insomnia
And sticking to all those duplicated mornings
I used to wake up and practice my laughs and practice my cries
With a duplicated mirror
I used to put my impatient signature in the bottom of official papers
I used to look for one thing in all the newspapers impatiently
And I used to come back from the office in all the afternoons of impatience
Coming back to the silence that welcomes you in every room
Coming back to the cold hands that keep the hot cup of tea
Coming back to the bad days followed by worse
And Coming back to me waiting to welcome my husband
Like a happy wife who waits to welcome her husband
Waiting for him to throw his socks in the living room
- run
My house is filled with the thrown away sounds
- run
Someone touched my shoulder
You should run to the streets of madding crowd
And to a woman in Arabian veil
You should run to those two shadows behind you

And to the fear of keeping a green wrist band in your hand
You should run to yourself stung by a hot bullet
And to your fingers of the V sign
You should run to the clotting blood in the corner of our lips
And to the night which is our sad resumption
To the incomplete night of liberty
And to yourself dying in my arms
To yourself being alive among the deads
And to our hands meeting each other again
Call me
I am you
I am as cold as your hands
Call me
I want to come back to the streets
Call me to whisper in your ears with love
Call me to lose myself in your arms and in my dreams
Come back and resurrect the memoires
Call me
And rescue me from myself.

Fatemeh Ekhtesari

Sentenced: 2015 (in exile)

Translated from Persian by Mohammad Hosseini Moghaddam

Daniil Kharms wrote stories for children and was a poet. He was known for his absurdist writings and his eccentricity, and it is said he died of starvation in a Soviet prison in 1942, possibly when he was sent into internal exile in Siberia. Kharms published around twelve popular books of children's stories, alongside prose and poetry between 1928 and 1941. Loved for his bizarre and irrational short tales containing dreamlike sequences and moments of comedy, Kharms openly claimed not to like children. Writing for them did, however, enable a freedom that became increasingly difficult through the 1930s under the Stalin-era socialist realism imposed on writers, as well as the persecution of non-conformist writers. Kharms founded the Union of Real Art – OBERIU. Between 1926 and 1930, OBERIU brought together avant-garde writers, most of whom were subsequently imprisoned or exiled. Kharms was sent into internal exile for several months in 1931. His banishment was believed to be because of a poem. He returned to make a meagre living through his writings until his arrest in 1941. Charged with 'libellous and defeatist' sentiments for his fierce refusal to be conscripted into the Red Army, he is said to have feigned madness to escape the death sentence. Instead, he was held in a prison psychiatric ward where he died in 1942, among the more than 1.5 million civilian victims during the Nazi Siege of Leningrad between 1941 and 1944.

The Brave Hedgehog

On the table there stood a box.
The animals approached the box, and started to examine, smell, and lick it.
And the box suddenly – one, two, three – and popped open.
And from the box – one, two, three – popped out a snake.
The animals got scared and ran off.
Only the hedgehog didn't get scared and yelled: "Kukareku!"
No, not that way! The hedgehog yelled: "Af-afaf!"
No, not like that either! The hedgehog yelled: "Meow-meow-meow!"
No, again not like that! I myself don't know how.
Who knows; how do hedgehogs scream?

Daniil Kharms

Imprisoned: 1931, 1942 (died in prison, in the psychiatric ward)

Translated from Russian by Alexander Cigale

Ashraf Fayadh is of Palestinian origin and was born in a refugee camp. He is a poet and artist. In 2016, he was sentenced in Saudi Arabia to eight years in prison and 800 lashes for apostasy. Fayadh is among a new generation of contemporary Saudi artists. He is a member of a British-Saudi art group and has curated several exhibitions, including one in Jeddah and another at the Venice Biennale in 2013. That year, he had an argument in a café with another artist on the subject of contemporary Saudi art, in which he was accused of having made 'blasphemous' comments. In trying to prove his 'illicit' and apostate behaviour, the authorities cited his long hair and smoking, as well as photos on his phone of Fayadh meeting women, said to be fellow artists. Also presented as evidence was his 2008 poetry collection, *Instructions Within*, which was published in Beirut and banned in Saudi Arabia. In 2015, he was sentenced to death by beheading. This was reduced to eight years' imprisonment in 2016. *Instructions Within* is Fayadh's only published collection of poetry and includes poems reflecting on the experience of refugees and displacement. Fayadh does not have Saudi citizenship. Since his imprisonment, his poetry has become internationally known, translated widely and published abroad as part of a campaign for his release.

The Last of the Line of Refugee Descendants

...

Being a refugee means standing at the end of the line
to get a fraction of a country.
Standing is something your grandfather did, without knowing the reason.
And the fraction is you.
Country: a card you put in your wallet with your money.
Money: pieces of paper with pictures of leaders.
Pictures: they stand in for you until you return.
Return: a mythical creature that appears in your grandfather's stories.
Here endeth the first lesson.
The lesson is conveyed to you so that you can learn the second lesson, which is
'what do you signify?'

...

Ashraf Fayadh

Imprisoned: 2013

Huang Xiang was born into a family of landowners whose land was seized by the Chinese communists in 1948 during the revolutionary war. His father was a member of the defeated Kuomintang. He was executed in 1949 when Huang was eight. Because of his social class, Huang was denied schooling, so he became self-taught, through the books left to him by his father. By his late teens, Huang's poems had been published in a state-approved journal but when, in 1958, a love poem by him was discovered, he was arrested for 'counter revolution'. From then until 1995, he was to spend a total of twelve years in prisons and labour camps for his poetry and activism. He was involved in the 1978–1979 'Democracy Wall Movement'. A calligrapher, Huang pasted large posters with big characters protesting human rights abuses on Mao Tse Tsung's mausoleum in Tiananmen Square, and posted an open letter to the US president Jimmy Carter the following year. The title of Huang's 1960 poem, *Singing Solo*, which is political and in free verse, implies a celebration of individualism that was prohibited in China, and could lead to a prison sentence. Huang's poetry is still banned in China. Several collections have been published abroad in translation since Huang and his wife left for exile in the US in 1997, where they remain today.

Singing Solo

Who am I
I am the lonely ghost of a waterfall
A poem
Living apart from the crowd forever
My drifting song follows an itinerant
Dream
My only audience
Silence

Huang Xiang

Imprisoned: several occasions, 1958–1995

Translated from Chinese by Michelle Yeh

Osip Mandelstam

One of Russia's greatest poets, **Osip Mandelstam** was a critic of the Soviet leader Josef Stalin. He died in 1938, en route to a Gulag camp. He was forty-seven. Mandelstam's poetry was first published in 1913. His writings bore witness to the repression of Stalin's regime. In 1933, a time when it was extremely dangerous to speak out even inside private homes for fear of informants, Mandelstam read aloud his poem, *Stalin's Epigram*, which fiercely mocked the leader, at gatherings of his friends. Described by a critic as '16 lines of a death sentence', the poem was never published for fear of repercussions. Mandelstam was arrested in 1934. Apparently with an eye on his image abroad, Stalin chose not to execute the poet, but to 'isolate and protect' him by sending him into internal exile. He stayed there until his release and return to Moscow in 1937. Three years in the Gulag had left Mandelstam in a state of physical and psychological collapse, so much so that when he was rearrested in 1938, he did not survive the journey to the labour camp and died in transit. His wife, at great risk to herself, memorised and preserved his manuscripts, and was eventually able to clandestinely republish them in the 1960s.

Stalin's Epigram

We live without feeling our country's pulse,
We can't hear ourselves, no one hears us,
If a word is uttered by chance,
Kremlin highlander is remembered at once.
Like worms his thick fingers are fat,
His words like pound weights are correct,
His cockroach moustache is full of laughter,
His army boots shine, he is sought after

By a mob of thin-necked leaders, half-men,
He uses their service, manipulating them:
Some are meowing or whistling, or whining,
He alone is poking, boking, and winning.
Like horseshoes, he grants his every decree
Poking some in the groin, in the brow, in the eye.
His executions are like cakes and ale,
His broad chest of Ossete eclipses the jail.

Osip Mandelstam

Internal exile: 1934–1937; died in transit: 1938

Translated from Russian by Ian Probstein

Mahmoud Darwish, regarded as the Palestinian national poet, spent most of his life in exile. Born in Western Galilee, Darwish's family were victims of the 1948 Arab–Israeli war, living as 'internal refugees' after losing their land. Darwish started writing poetry in the 1960s and was politically active from a young age, for which he was arrested several times. His poem, *Identity Card*, was a diatribe directed at an Israeli policeman, and it became a popular protest song, leading to his house arrest. In 1970, Darwish left Israel to study in Moscow. He then lived as an exile in Tunisia, Egypt, Lebanon and France, working as a journalist and editor while writing. He returned to Ramallah in the mid-1990s. Initially, he was a member of the Israeli Communist Party. Between 1987 and 1993, he was on the Executive Committee of the Palestinian Liberation Organisation and drafted its manifesto for independence in 1988. Critical of both Israeli and Palestinian leadership, he was admired for his defence of, and belief in, peace. He maintained that eventually peace would be possible. He published more than thirty collections of poetry, as well as eight novels, winning numerous awards, and large audiences attended his readings.

Identity Card

Write down:
I am an Arab.
My ID card number is 50,000.
My children: eight
And the ninth is coming after the summer.
Are you angry?

*
Write down:
I am an Arab.
I work with my toiling comrades in a quarry.
My children are eight,
And out of the rocks
I draw their bread,
Clothing and writing paper.
I do not beg for charity at your door
Nor do I grovel
At your doorstep tiles.
Does that anger you?

*
Write down:
I am an Arab,
A name without a title,
Patient in a country where everything
Lives on flared-up anger.
My roots...
Took firm hold before the birth of time,
Before the beginning of the ages,
Before the cypress and olives,
Before the growth of pastures.
My father...of the people of the plow,
Not of noble masters.
My grandfather, a peasant
Of no prominent lineage,
Taught me pride of self before reading of books.
My house is a watchman's hut
Of sticks and reed.
Does my status satisfy you?
I am a name without a title

*
Write down:
I am an Arab.
Hair coal-black,

Eyes brown,
My distinguishing feature:
On my head a koufiyah topped by the igal,
And my palms, rough as stone,
Scratch anyone who touches them.
My address:
An unarmed village – forgotten –
Whose streets are nameless,
And all its men are in the field and quarry.
Are you angry?

*

Write down:
I am an Arab
Robbed of my ancestors' vineyards
And of the land cultivated
By me and all my children.
Nothing is left for us and my grandchildren
Except these rocks...
Will your government take them too, as reported?
Therefore,
Write at the top of page one:
I do not hate people,
I do not assault anyone,
But...if I get hungry,
I eat the flesh of my usurper.
Beware...beware...of my hunger,
And of my anger.

Mahmoud Darwish

Exiled: 1970s–1990s

Translated from Arabic by Salman Hilmy

Yannis Ritsos, who fought against the fascist regime in Greece, is one of the country's most popular and widely translated poets of the twentieth century. In the early 1930s, Ritsos joined the Communist Party of Greece, around the same time as his poetry collection, *Tractor,* was published. This was to be the first of more than hundred volumes of poetry, novels and stage plays he published over his lifetime. His early poetry reflected his communist beliefs. One of the most popular, *Epiphanies* (O Epitaphios), published in 1936, was inspired by the assassination of a worker during a general strike. It was among Ritsos's books that were symbolically burned by right-wing government supporters before the Temple of Zeus at the Acropolis. When civil war broke out between the communists and the right-wing government in 1944, Ritsos went underground. He was arrested when the communists were defeated in 1949 and spent four years in prison. Under the military junta which ruled Greece from 1967 to 1974, Ritsos was again interned on the Greek islands, then placed under house arrest in Athens. While on the island prisons, he was denied paper. But he wrote hundreds of poems on fragments of wood and stones. Despite the turbulence of his life, he continued to write, completing more than a hundred books, including plays and essays.

Tomorrow Maybe They Will Kill Us

We smile inside.
That smile, we hide now.
Illegal smile,
as now the sun has been illegal,
illegal, also, the truth.
We hide the smile, the way we hide in our pocket,
the photograph of our beloved,
as we hide the idea of freedom,
between the two leaves of our heart.
We all have the same sky and the same smile.

Tomorrow maybe they will kill us.
Tomorrow maybe they will kill us.
This smile, and this sky, they cannot take from us.
This smile,
This smile,
This smile, and this sky, they cannot take from us.

Yannis Ritsos

Imprisoned: 1946–1950, 1967–1974

Translated from Greek

Missing since 2001.
Amanuel Asrat

On 23 September 2001, thirty-year-old poet and songwriter **Amanuel Asrat** was taken away from his home in Eritrea by government forces. He has not been seen since. It is not known whether he is alive. Asrat was among eleven people working for independent newspapers who were seized that day under a crackdown against government critics. Nothing has been heard of them since. Prison conditions in Eritrea are known to be dire, with many reports of torture. In 2016, a leaked report said that Asrat was held in Eiraeiro Prison, and later that he had been transferred to an unknown place elsewhere. Asrat's family continues to press for news of his fate, and, if still alive, for him to be freed. But the Eritrean government has refused comment. A popular poet and songwriter, Asrat wrote on war and peace, and on the plight of the under-privileged. His poem, *The Scourge of War*, won a national prize. He wrote for the *Zemen* newspaper, known for its focus on arts and literature. Months before his arrest, as part of a circle of writers, he had founded the grassroots Saturday's Supper literary clubs, which were set up across Eritrea.

The Scourge of War

Where two brothers pass each other
Where two brothers meet each other
Where two brothers conjoin
In the piazza of life and death
In the gulf of calamity and cultivation
In the valley of fear and peace
Something resounded.

The ugliness of the thing of war
When its spring comes
When its ravaging echoes knock at your door
It is then that the scourge of war brews doom
But…
You serve it willy-nilly
Unwillingly you keep it company
Still, for it to mute how hard you pray!

Amanuel Asrat

Imprisoned: 2001 to date

Translated from Tigrinya by Tedros Abraham in collaboration with David Shook

The leading Caribbean poet **Martin Carter** of Guyana was deeply engaged in politics, for which he was twice imprisoned. Carter was a member of the socialist People's Progressive Party (PPP) that won elections in May 1953. However, the party's victory was short-lived. In October, the British government placed what was then British Guiana under emergency law, and Carter was arrested. He was held without charge until January 1954, only to be imprisoned again in June that year for taking part in a protest. He was held in an army detention centre for six months. After his release, his poems written in jail were published in one of his best-known collections, *Poems of Resistance from British Guiana*. Carter was the first poet to write on slavery, Amerindian history and Indian indentureship from a contemporary perspective. His first book of poetry was published in 1951. When Guyana gained independence in 1966, Carter became a government minister, acting as the country's United Nations representative. A year later, disillusioned with internal political factions, he resigned from politics altogether. He published numerous collections throughout his life, gaining respect for his passionate reflections on struggle and resistance.

A Banner for the Revolution

This is my hand
for the revolution........

that night there will be thousands of torches
from the hospitals the lame will come
the mad will be sane again
for the revolution.

those who cannot read
will learn to read
for the revolution –
those who despair not
will be glad
for the revolution –
those who are eager to be men
will be glad
for the revolution –
I myself shall be so fiercely happy
that I will make my shirt
a banner
for the revolution,
a banner
for the revolution.

Martin Carter

Imprisoned: 1953 and 1954

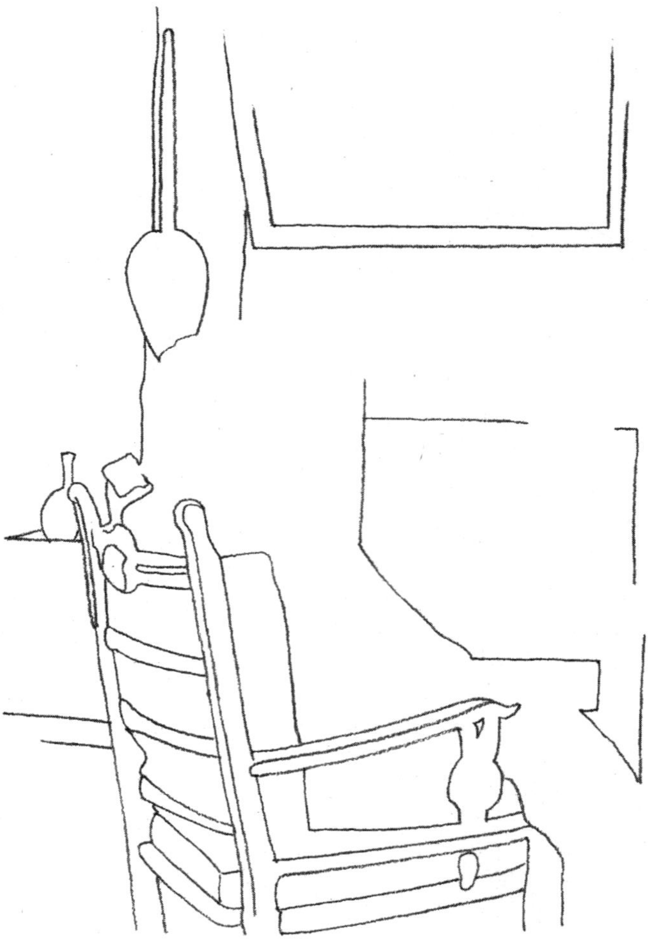

Nâzim Hikmet

Described as a 'romantic revolutionary', **Nâzım Hikmet**, Turkey's most renowned poet of the twentieth century, spent much of his life in prison or in exile. Hikmet was a Marxist, and began publishing poems as a young man, the first being celebrations of the war of independence, which received praise from modern Turkey's founding father, Kemal Ataturk. After spending a year studying in Moscow, he returned in 1924 to work with leftist magazines, which published his poems and articles. His poem *City of No Voice*, written in support of the taxi-drivers' strike against the Istanbul municipality's decision to reduce fares, was published anonymously in the literary journal *Resimli Ay* in 1929. The journal's director was sentenced to ten years in prison and a fine. A campaign against Nâzım Hikmet was then started by fellow prominent writers accusing him of communist propaganda. He was sentenced to fifteen years in 1925, although he escaped to Russia, returning to Turkey in 1928 following an amnesty. He went on to write a large body of poetry, plays and film scripts. In 1938, Hikmet was again imprisoned, this time for provoking rebellion on a naval ship. The sole evidence against him was that his poetry was read by military cadets. Sentenced to twenty-eight years in prison, he was released under an amnesty in 1950. He left Turkey to live in Russia, where he remained until his death in 1965.

City of No Voice

Revolutions per minute*
zero.
The city
shut up
The asphalt-cement jaws
of the dot dot city
locked up in the dot dot year
dot dot
month...
The street is empty
run from one end to the other.
There is nothing in the street
lmy pockets alike...
Water's cut, no water running...
no engine humming
no wheel turning.
The wind:
is dragging mister ford's name on to the asphalt:
blowing a sheet of notice
on the pavement...
Three men
three men are standing:
One is carrying a broken
violin,
the second is wearing a cylindrical hat
and a frock coat,
The third, like a hairy ape, is naked...
Street.
Whistling
rubbing your neck
you could just walk across the street.
No fear of being run over
no engine humming
no wheel turning
The wind:
Frowning its eyebrows more and more.
sounds of tooting are now the gatekeepers.
Three men...
three men are standing
and a drunkard singing a folk song
hitting his heels on the road...

* 'Revolutions per minute.' One other reason why Nâzım was accused of communist propaganda is the pun on the word 'Devir', which both means 'turn, revolve' for the engine of the car, and 'to knock something over, to overthrow the government, subversion'.

Stop screaming in the street
stop hitting your heels on the road
In vain.
You cannot make the asphalt find its tongue!
In vain.
The city that lost its voice cannot talk
if their hands
locked in their pockets
do not stroke
the copper wires…
Three men:
three men are standing:
One is carrying a broken
violin,
the second is wearing a cylindrical hat
and a frock coat,
the third, like a hairy ape, is naked…
Three men vanishing
swaying in the dark…

Nâzim Hikmet

Imprisoned: 1924, 1938–1950

Translated from Turkish by Yusuf Eradam

Tommaso Campanella was a philosopher, writer and poet who spent more than half his life in Italian prisons in the late sixteenth and early seventeenth centuries for his heretical views. A friar who entered the Dominican order in 1583, Campanella was a follower of Bernardino Telesio, a pioneer of modern empiricism, and defended his contemporary Galileo. Both men were considered heretics by the Catholic church. He was himself imprisoned in 1594 for three years for heresy. Then, in 1599, he was arrested again, tortured and accused of a plot to overthrow Spanish rule in his home region of Calabria. Sentenced to life imprisonment, he was held for twenty-seven years in various prison fortresses, before his release. After one of his followers was implicated in another conspiracy, he fled to France in 1634. He died in Paris in 1639. Campanella wrote throughout his long imprisonment, producing numerous books. The best-known, *City of the Sun*, promoted an egalitarian society where undue wealth and poverty are non-existent, and all property is held in common. Few of his poems survive. He is considered one of the original pioneers in Italian literature.

A Sonnet Written for One Who Died by the Holy Office in Rome

Soul, who has just departed the gloomy prison
of this world, of Italy, and of Rome,
of the Inquisition and the mortal coil,
go to Heaven, for we will follow after you.

...

Tommaso Campanella

Imprisoned: 1599–1626

Translated from Italian by Sherry Roush

In 2011, the student activist **Ayat al-Qurmezi** was imprisoned. She was beaten and tortured for reading a poem of resistance against the Bahraini regime. In February that year, Bahraini protestors gathered in the streets of the capital, Manama, calling for regime change. They were part of the Arab uprisings that had sprung up that year. In March, thousands in Bahrain were arrested and around thirty-five were killed. Al-Qurmezi was a student at the Bahrain faculty of teaching. She had taken to the platform at the Pearl Roundabout, the hub of the protests. There, she read out her poem, which contained the lines: 'We are people who kill humiliation and who assassinate injustice.' Videos of her reading were spread across the internet. Learning that she would be arrested, al-Qurmezi went into hiding in mid-March. She gave herself up at the end of the month on hearing that her family home had been raided by the police, who threatened to kill her brothers unless she came forward. She spent sixteen days in prison, during which time she suffered beatings and electric shocks. Brought to trial on 12 June, she was sentenced to a year's imprisonment. She was freed a month later to serve the rest of her sentence under house arrest.

Khalifa*

Hear me:
You, the elder,
the 'good man', who 'safeguards justice'
(so you have always declared),

if I were to make excuses for you,
I, for you,
for the things you have done,
I would only look the fool,
for you would continue in your ways,
and murder us as 'traitors'.

Hear me:
Hear us all, for we all demand likewise -
both sects, all Bahrainis:

You must go.
Take His Majesty with you,
and leave your deeds behind.

You, oppressor,
from where do you derive your power,
the power to keep your people down? -
all your people,
even women
even children
even men.
Yet you call for 'dialogue',
even in the midst of your brutality?

No! ... No! ...
One word: No!
One demand:
Give us back our Bahrain.
Return this country to its people;
to us, its people.

Our Bahrain is ours.

Ayat al-Qurmezi

Imprisoned: 2011

Translated from Arabic by Ghias Aljundi with Mitchell Albert

* Prime minister

Ajmal Khattak was a political leader, an avowed Marxist and Pashtun nationalist, who wrote revolutionary poetry from an early age. He was born in 1925 and took part in the freedom movement for Pakistan, and he wrote in Pashto. He went on to become a leading figure in Pakistani politics. He was a prominent member of the left-leaning, secular Awami National Party (ANP), which stood for Pashtun nationalism. He fled into exile in Afghanistan when the party was banned in 1973, returning sixteen years later. He went on to become a member of the Pakistan National Assembly, and was president of the ANP. Khattak wrote several books of poetry and Pashto literature that revolted against social and political deprivation. In 1953, he was imprisoned for nine months. He said he had been tortured to force him to confess to being part of a plot to overthrow the government. When Khattak died in 2010, thousands of mourners crowded the streets to attend his funeral. Khattak was a religious scholar - he wrote critically of the hypocrisy of some religious leaders, such as in his poem *Paradise*. Even after death, he continued to be the target of the ire of religious extremists who, in 2012, partly destroyed his mausoleum, attempting to blow it up.

Wishes

So many are the wishes in my heart
How I pray your liquid eyes to fulfill them all

Each drop of my tears is a piece of my heart
filled with countless regrets

Ask not my mouth, ask rather my eyes, red with tears
Filled with a rainbow of prayerful longings

Waiting for a single smiling glance from a certain person
I have books full of wishes

As provisions for this world and the next, O Khattak,
I have burnt spots on my injured heart

Ajmal Khattak

Imprisoned: 1953

Translated from Pashto by Najib Manalai

César Vallejo is considered to be one of the most illustrious poets of the twentieth century. He published three collections of poetry in his lifetime, lived in poverty and exile. In 1920, Vallejo was inadvertently caught up in a political feud when he was accused of committing arson at a businessman's home. He went into hiding for three months before being arrested and imprisoned. He was temporarily released in February 1921. Although it was clear that the evidence against him had been falsified, it was only in 2007 that he was vindicated by the Peruvian judiciary as having been 'falsely accused'. Fearing re-imprisonment, Vallejo left Peru in 1923 for exile in Europe, where he lived in poverty and suffered from poor health. He never returned home. Described as a tragic and passionate poet whose writings are a testimony to human pain, his work was influenced by his experience working on a sugar plantation as a young man, his time in prison and in exile, and the Spanish Civil War.

The Tennis Player in the Moment

The tennis player in the moment
at which he masterfully serves the ball
is possessed by a wholly animal innocence;
the philosopher in the moment when he apprehends a new truth
is a perfect beast.
Anatole France maintained
that a religious feeling is the by-product
of a special organ in the human body,
till now unknown, and thus
it could also be said
that in the very moment at which such an organ
were fully employed,
so free of malice would a believer be
that one could almost consider him a vegetable.
Oh soul! Oh thought! Oh Marx! Oh Feuerbach!

César Vallejo

Imprisoned: 1920–1921

Translated from Spanish by Dave Bonta

Faiz Ahmad Faiz is a revered revolutionary poet and political figure who spent periods in exile and prison in Pakistan. He wrote in Urdu and Punjabi, and published many books and articles, including eight volumes of poetry, two of which were written in prison. His work reflects Pakistan's turbulent history from the 1940s to the 1980s. After serving in the British Army during the Second World War, Faiz threw himself into politics, becoming a founding member of the Communist Party of Pakistan in 1947. He was also a leader of Pakistan's trade union movement through the 1940s and 1950s. In 1951, Faiz got entangled in a failed coup attempt led by left-wing military leaders. He served four years in prison, then left Pakistan, returning in 1958. He was again arrested, this time for his pro-communist publications. As editor of the left-leaning *Pakistan Times,* he had contributed articles and poems critical of the government. Released in 1960, he again went into exile, returning to take up the invitation to join Zulfikar Ali Bhutto's government as cultural advisor. He resigned in 1974. In 1979, Bhutto was executed. Faiz, fearing arrest, went into exile again, this time to Lebanon, and returned to Pakistan in 1982, when war broke out there.

Speak

Speak, for your lips are free;
Speak, your tongue is still yours,
Your upright body is yours –
Speak, your life is still yours.
See how in the blacksmith's shop
The flames are hot, the iron is red,
Mouths of locks have begun to open,
Each chain's skirt has spread wide.

Speak, this little time is plenty
Before the death of body and tongue:
Speak, for truth is still alive –
Speak, say whatever is to be said.

Faiz Ahmad Faiz

Imprisoned: 1951 and 1958

Translated from Urdu by V.G. Kiernan

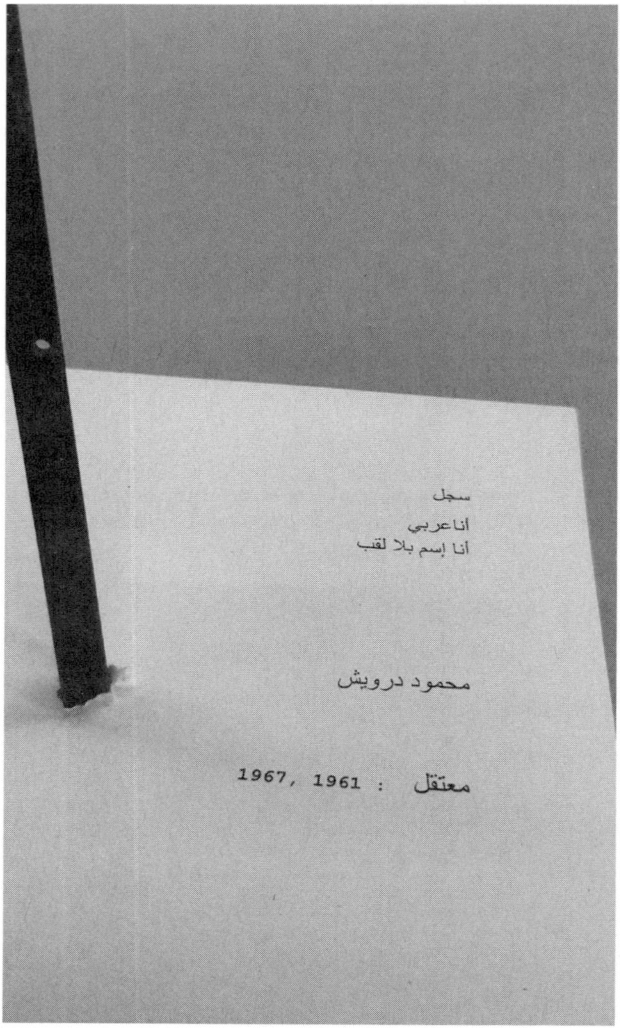
سجل
أناعربي
أنا إسم بلا لقب
محمود درويش
معتقل : 1961, 1967

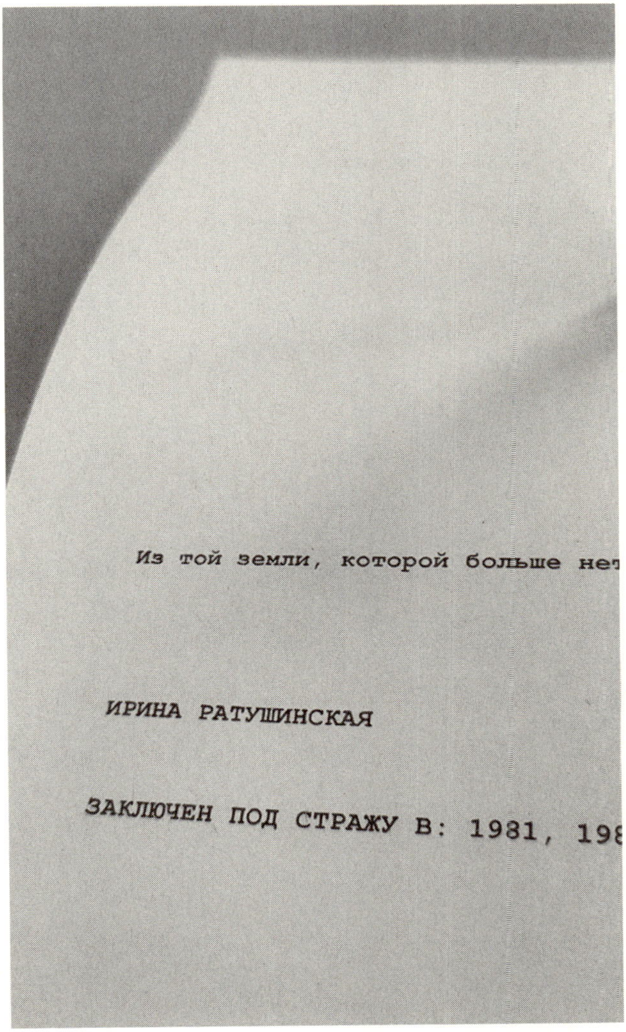
Из той земли, которой больше нет
ИРИНА РАТУШИНСКАЯ
ЗАКЛЮЧЕН ПОД СТРАЖУ В: 1981, 198

دیپ جس کا محلات ہی میں جلے
چاند لوگوں کی خوشیوں کو لے کر چلے
وہ جو سائے میں ہر مشکلات کے پلے
ایسے دستور کو صبح و بے نور کو
میں نہیں مانتا، میں نہیں جانتا

حبیب جلیب

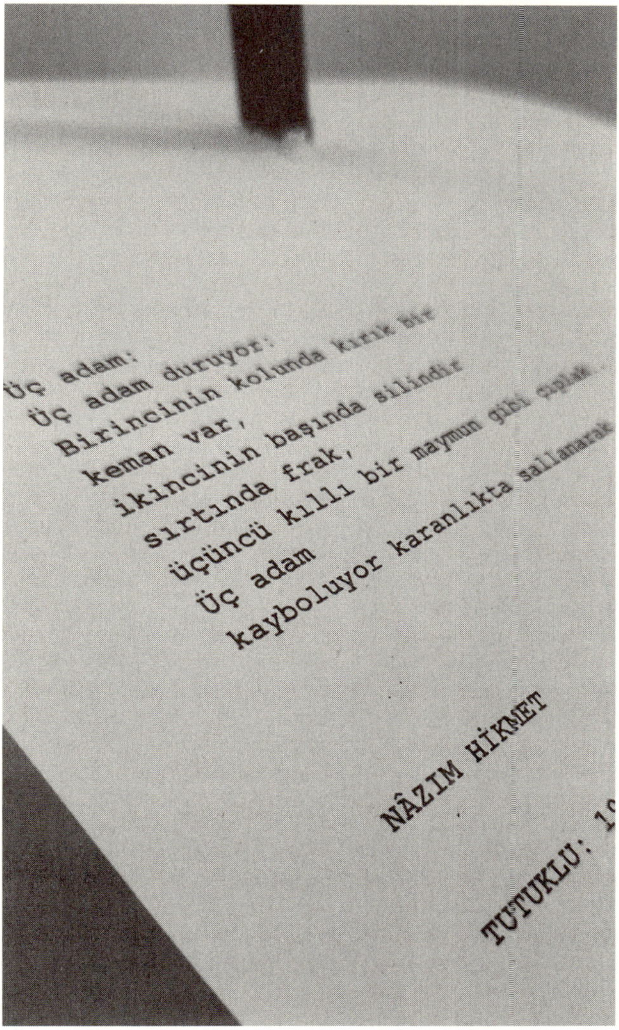
Üç adam:
Üç adam duruyor:
Birincinin kolunda kırık bir
keman var,
ikincinin başında silindir
sırtında frak,
üçüncü kıllı bir maymun gibi çıplak
Üç adam
kayboluyor karanlıkta sallanarak
NÂZIM HİKMET
TUTUKLU:

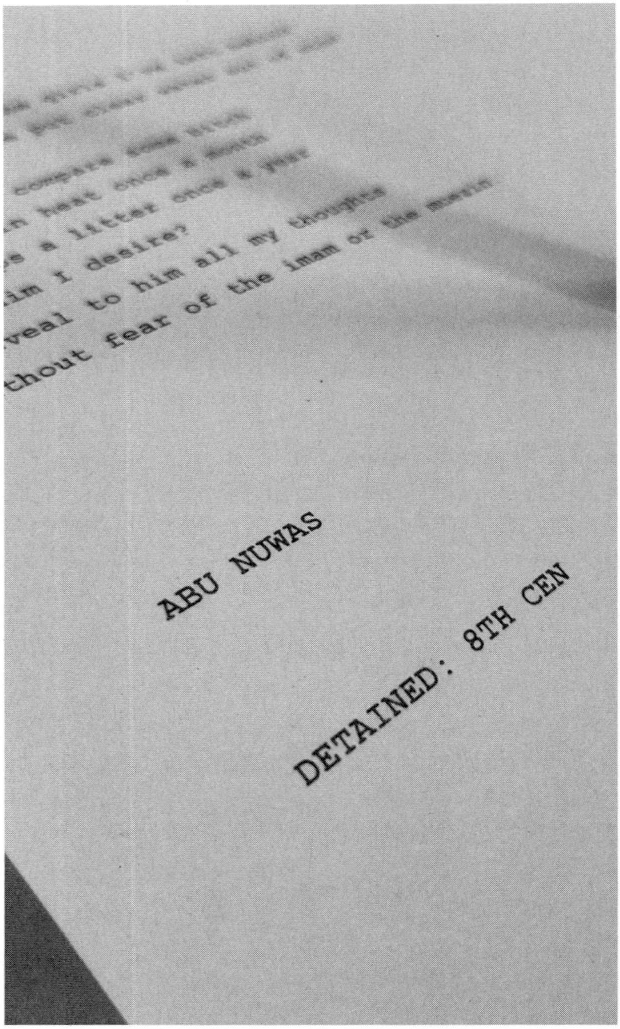

s a litter once a year
im I desire?
veal to him all my thoughts
thout fear of the imam
ABU NUWAS
DETAINED: 8TH CEN

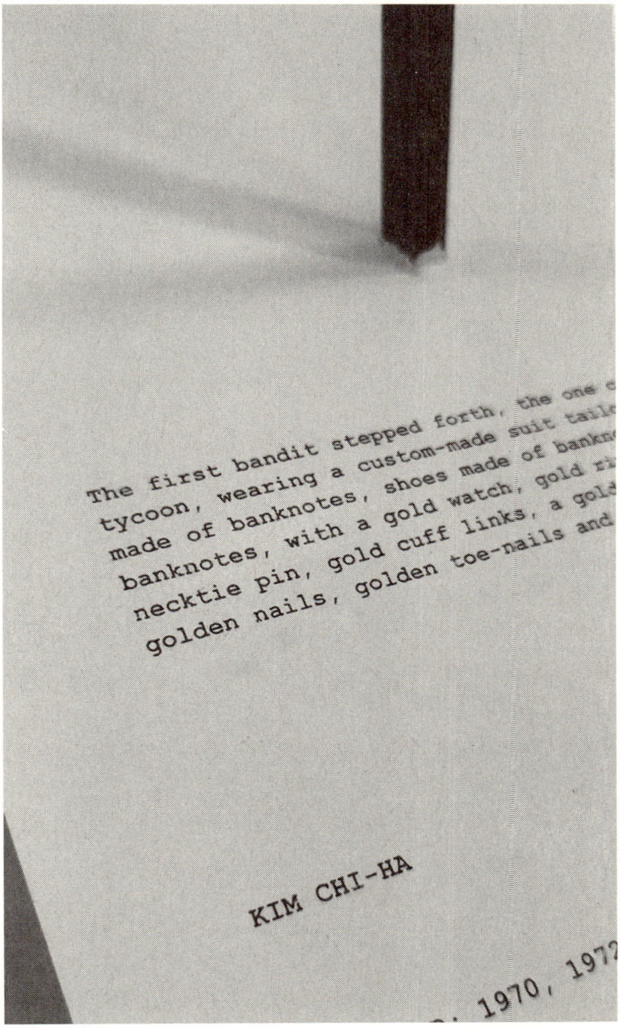
The first bandit stepped forth, the one
tycoon, wearing a custom-made suit
made of banknotes, shoes made of
banknotes, with a gold watch, gold
necktie pin, gold cuff links, a
golden nails, golden toe-nails and
KIM CHI-HA
1970,

It's Forbidden to Give Pens to Prisoners, Especially to You

Dareen Tatour

Translated from Arabic by Lauren Pyott

The hours pass slowly in captivity. Cockroaches and bedbugs were my only companions in this cell in the Jalameh detention centre. I tried to keep myself occupied with the insects to distract my ears from the ceaseless sound of the dripping tap, along with my constant heavy coughing. I painstakingly traced their movements on the wall and was deeply moved by the fact that these cockroaches, here in this prison, knew nothing of hibernation or rest. They paid no heed to the place they found themselves in, nor to the cold that surrounded them, and me. These insects moving in front of me were the only sure proof that there was life at all in this bleak cell. Whenever the hours stretched while I was alone in solitary confinement, and I missed having someone to talk to, I looked at these small insects and struck up a conversation with them. That was enough to relieve the burden of my loneliness and keep me from surrendering to despair or frustration.

In prison, every time my sense of alienation intensified, I would redefine the smallest details around me from scratch, probably in a different way to any other prisoner or detainee. I managed to discover a new philosophy of feeling, for prison really does offer a philosophy that triggers the eyes of memory, when the prisoner is a poet or a photographer.

Light always starts from a narrow hole. I summoned these thoughts to create some value and importance to my current life, here in my dark hole, rearranging my mind so I could be reborn with hope and faith. I convinced myself that even if I died after this harsh experience, there could be no doubt that I died for my values and principles.

I sat on the bed with a tentative sense of calm, filled with thoughts of waiting, and unable to do anything but analyse. It was down to me to leave this narrow spot by stealth, through my imagination.

Lots of things written on the wall intrigued me, and I started to read and examine them: various phrases in Arabic, Hebrew and English; the names of people who had passed through here; a picture of a heart; a love arrow with initials; prayers and insults. I would read them – sometimes laughing, sometimes lamenting – and would empathise with whoever had written the phrase. I wished that I had my camera with me to photograph this rare painting, and felt an even stronger need for a pen, and for writing itself.

I asked for pen and paper, but the prison guard refused to give me anything. I tried to understand the reason, her plea that it was prohibited by law here. Immediately I asked her about the writings on the wall, and where they had come from. My reply surprised her and her face bore the shock of my question. I remained quiet and she said again: 'These are the rules here. It's forbidden to give pens to prisoners, especially to you.' She withdrew from the discussion and left without answering my question. I returned to the bed with a volcano of anger at this ridiculous reply, and at the sham of such rules. But at that moment, I suppressed my anger, and a new fact dawned on me that brought overwhelming joy, making me smile. Overcoming anger was a triumph in this moment, and the guard's retreat from the conversation was a victory of another kind over the system I faced in prison.

More hours passed and all I could do was think, read the writings on the wall, and pray. Prayer too is my sanctuary when I feel the need to speak to someone. I pray to God and speak to Him as though He is in front of me, believing in my heart that there is a message for me to deliver in my detention. This makes me satisfied with everything, and I thank God for that, and wait to find out what the message is behind my detainment and imprisonment. My trust in God and my immense faith helped me contain myself, bit by bit.

My deprivation continued to be one of the most precious things in my life: no pen or paper, a cell in which I lost my dignity by degree, and lived beyond time and place. I reached the furthest point of boredom, frustration, despair and anxiety, and was nearly driven to madness by all that surrounded me. When I started to feel the emptiness of my existence, and the onset of a breakdown, I transformed into a different person. I would rave and talk to myself out loud the whole time, to relieve the pressure of that irritating sound of dripping water. Sometimes I would scream so as to forget, other times I would sing to distract myself from sickness and coughing. Then I would dance and laugh out loud whenever the non-political prisoners approached the door with their cigarettes, exhaling their smoke into my cell in full view of the warden. They would see my indifference and on hearing the word 'crazy' from them, I would intensify my singing and dancing and coughing. And the strange thing is that I didn't cry once, despite all the pain that gripped me throughout the time I was alone.

I reached a point when I could no longer bear this humiliation, this emptiness, this nihilism. My thoughts began to refuse the lifestyle that prison had imposed on me, as well as the conditions of this grey cell. So I found myself evoking memories of bygone days, and would compare what I would have been doing in a similar moment when I was on the outside, to what I was experiencing in this solitary cell, and I would try to focus on whatever I might have been doing then.

I remembered my love for jogging, so I would spend my day walking in the cell, as much as the space would allow, from the toilet to the door, to-ing and fro-ing. Walking like this was how I avoided succumbing to the tyranny of time, or of collapsing into the fatal despair that was taking hold of me.

I would imagine that the grey walls were the road I loved walking on in the streets of Nazareth, leading to the old market quarter. In this way, I would walk up and down in the cell for long hours. The prison guard would approach, stop at the door and ask me: 'What are you up to?'

But I wouldn't give any reply and would complete my imaginary tour of Nazareth. She too would cast the word 'crazy' at me and leave.

Every time I felt I was an isolated and confined prisoner, I would give myself a talking to, saying: 'I am a prisoner for the sake of freedom.' And I would feel that freedom was imprisoned in me too, living and residing inside of me. Whenever I became overwhelmed with feelings of sadness, pain and restriction, I would imagine Freedom as a woman like myself, right in front of me. I would strike up a conversation and would hear her chiding me, saying: 'You, Dareen, are free.' I would start to sing to her and to myself, and would hear her respond to my singing, and my voice: 'Dareen, you are the sound of freedom, can't you hear freedom's call? You are the sound of freedom.' The smaller I felt my cell was, the greater was my freedom.

I sat on the bed and tried to sleep, but couldn't. I had a severe, unbearable headache and had no option but to ask the prison guard for a painkiller. An hour after my request, she handed me a yellow Acamol pill. I took it and returned to the bed, and quite out of my norm, started to examine the tablet, then rolled it between my palms. Every time I went to swallow it, I would imagine it was a pen, and so reconsidered. Suddenly I had an intense desire to write. A strong urge for a pen overcame me and I could no longer stand myself without writing. All I could feel was my fingers gripping the tablet in an effort to write with it on the wall. My attempt failed, yielding no results. I placed the tablet in my palms and went back to looking at it closely, willing it to somehow release its ink.

I felt a little cold and pulled up the zip on my jacket, then quickly tore it off me, separating the zip, and tried to write with it on the wall. Success. My name, date and time were the first things I wrote. Then my hand inscribed my first prison poem.

It Would Not Have Been

Muhammad al-Faqih Saleh[14]

1953–2017

Translated from Arabic by Khaled Mattawa

(Translator's note: In 2012, shortly after the rebellion that toppled Col. Muammar Qaddafi, a 1986 resentencing verdict issued by the Permanent Revolutionary Court became public. In the document, the life sentence issued against the poet Muhammad al-Faqih Saleh *was changed to capital punishment, but for reasons never explained, the execution was not carried out.)*

It seems
that all that has happened to me
would not have been possible...

I would not have visited the countries I visited
or tasted their delicacies.
I would not have done all that insanity directed me to do.

I would not have desired the ones I desired.
Their paths would not have led me
to their mirages.
Nothing of them would have remained in my heart
except hidden delectable echoes.

I would not have been
father to my daughter
or achieved what I've achieved.
I would never have turned inward disappointed
every time defeats struck my free soul.

14. In 1978, the poet Muhammad al-Faqih Saleh was imprisoned along with a number of Libyan writers on charges of forming a leftist party aimed at overthrowing the regime in Libya. All accused were sentenced to life terms.

I would not have imbibed all that I could
of the ancestors' vintage words,
or immersed the bee of my soul
in the sweet nectars of art.

Old age would not have charged me
and pinned its gray banners to my crown.

Poetry would not have rattled me
or burned me with its stubborn flames.

I would not have quarreled with family and friends,
would not have known what I've known
of sorrow and wounds.

All that I have been through
would not have been possible
when someone thought he was too lenient
by allowing me remain alive
imprisoned
swallowing bitterness,
listening to the years passing by.

Writing Poems in Prison

Stella Nyanzi

Unjustly convicted and locked up in prison,
I was serving an eighteen-month sentence.
Preserving my sanity was the first reason
That drove me to write poems without repentance.
Dissidents are treated as if we committed treason.
My pen wrote about the total absence of lenience.
Writing rhythmic rhymes behind the bars of prison,
Allowed me to pour out emotion without pretence.

I wrote poems about the faded dream of liberation
And envisioned the new society full of freedom.
I ruthlessly criticised actors in our failed revolution
And analysed how their actions lacked wisdom.
Behind bars, I fought the constant consternation
By writing livid poems driving away the boredom.
When bereaved, poems brought me consolation.
Solitary grief in prison broke group rites of my kingdom.

Torn from my three teenaged children for months,
I fondly wrote motherly poems directed at my offspring.
Accused as a 'bad mother' by the magistrate's words,
Poems for my children were gut earnest outpourings.
Blamed by relatives for straying from my parents' paths,
Some poems recall father's wisdom and my mourning.
Retracing my mother's resolve, boldness and bounce,
I wrote poems exalting my heritage on prison floorings.

When prison wardresses tortured or wounded prisoners,
I wrote a poem to record this abuse of public office.
When prison wardresses denied prisoners meals all day,
I wrote a poem against the logic of group punishments.

When prison wardresses stole gifts from prison visitors,
I wrote a poem flagging this illegal profiteering.
When prison wardresses beat me up...
so bad
that I miscarried the baby in my womb...
I wrote poems to make sense of this senselessness.

Hearing the laughter ringing from the belly of a prisoner,
I wrote poems on the unending register of contradictions.
Receiving kindness from women convicted of murder,
My poems shattered stories of prison generalisations.
The freedom I enjoyed in prison often made me wonder
Causing me to write abundantly during this isolation.
Arrested, charged, tried, convicted, sentenced as a writer,
I used my incarceration to create a new poetry publication.

Between Two Cells

For Mazen Darwish, and all the prisoners of the Syrian regime

Yasser Khanjer[15]

Translated from Arabic by Marilyn Hacker

I hear your voice light up the next cell
and the question occurs to me
Where does the guard change his clothes
when he goes from your cell to mine?
How does he shift the letters on his lips
without one of the two 'enemy' languages breaking
– a language in despair since its creation,
gloomy since infancy, lame
oblique
deceitful
that manages, once it's beautified itself
to trap its neighbor, enthralled
in undoing the good-luck charms of its childhood
– a language with malleable meanings
engrossed by the charms of exegesis,
barefoot, like a dancer bent backwards,
her anklets linking the text's foot
to the sultan's desire.
How does he change the letters on his lips,
a guard who pronounces words badly
when he goes from my cell to yours?

*

Are you smoking?
Reach your hand out between the bars
I'll light your cigarette for you,

15. Yasser Khanjer was imprisoned from 1997 till 2005 by the Israeli occupation forces, on the charges of resisting the occupation.

the last one in the pack
Inhale its smoke in secret
so the guard doesn't take it away.
The light here is dim,
no star knows this wounded horizon.
Draw up a little sunlight from your heart,
it will gouge out the eye of darkness

*

The guard's face here, root of a chronic death
and mirror of a massacre there.
The guard's face there, bloody with defeats
he only describes in secret.
Since he hasn't learned the role of victim
he dresses in his wolf costume
to hunt down a letter in a poem and riddle it with wounds.
The guard's face there,
memory of a surrender heavy with stories

*

To the guards here and there, a weakness like dry grass
if each one weren't leaning on a rifle
that stands guard over the dunes of his fear,
a confession throbbing in a song.
And if they exchange a few insults
the aim is clear,
they are only juggling masks.
They are a pair of twins,
they have one umbilical cord,
there where their shadows fell on the earth
a slaughter follows a slaughter.
I hear your voice, the brushing of pine needles
as it climbs the steps of prayer
then exhales the perfectly baked bread of freedom
toward a heart open to the winds

To the prisoners here and those there
a single heart
that gets drunk on a breath of freedom

*

I have comrades in prison
who turn each night, penitent, towards pillows of hope
Hunger devours them
Thirst withers them
yet they persist in adorning the hip of our shattered age
with a flock of freed birds

In the Lonely Cool Before Dawn

Ma Thida

IN a room like my parent's womb, I eat silence while my heart fills with thunder. I want to say 'I' but the word has passed away. No one is here. Where are 'you' or 'he' or 'she'? He or she or you were here and near the room but they left here or passed away. I want to meet them anyway. How did they leave? Were they set free or forced to move somewhere? How did they disappear? I heard many stories about them and I think my story might be another. My room is alive with mice, ants, cockroaches and absence. Though I can keep away from those mysterious creatures, the absence doesn't go away. I breathe a sigh of relief. To breathe in means I am alive. I glance up expecting nothing but a ghost.

THE womb is filled with a forty-watt lightbulb. Starlight rains in every city, every country and every society. But there is a brick wall fence beyond my only window, which is guarded by a double layer of wooden sticks and iron bars. Barbed wire garlands the wall like a giant's crown. Oh! A flying ghost! Please come over the wire and through my so-called window into the womb. I want to say 'I' and 'You'. You have to just listen to me but do nothing. I'd like to offer you my property. The womb is only furnished with a piece of wooden plank, my bed. Oh! Never mind. You don't need to worry. I have two pots – one for drinking water and one for cleaning water – and two bowls – a small one as a plate at mealtime and a cup at bath time, and a big one as a toilet. Anyhow I like to share my things with you for tonight before dawn when you have to leave.

LONELY life! Loneliness is the poverty of self; solitude is the richness of self. I memorized what May Sarton wrote. Yes! I am alone but not lonely; I'll be all – the master and the staff, or the leader and the follower, or the teacher and the student. I order me to clean the room and I ask me to take some rest. The master I order and the staff I request rest. I agree with I and no one can convince both Is to refuse. So, I clean the womb and take rest. I tell me not to bow to the warders and I listen to me and do so. Though the warders don't like me, I like my leader who is me. I teach me to learn myself in order to know everything. I learn myself through meditation and by learning the self I understand the universe. To learn the self is to have no need for others, but to accept being alone. Sorry ghost! I need you no more. I need myself. Myself needs me. Yes, solitude is a kind of freedom. Did anyone who lived in this womb notice this?

COOL polluted air embraces me. Thin cotton blankets try to keep me warm. Learning how coolness feels makes me notice the impermanence of coolness. Coolness goes on and warmness goes in. I can be alive alone even in this cool womb. The weather is cool and the warders are cool-blooded beasts. But I can neglect them all. I already know what will happen in this world. We want to have a world where people's hearts are opened, their stomachs are filled, their wills are calmed and their needs are cleansed. We struggled to have this world but we have been drowned in the barred world. For me, it is the indifference between cold and warmth.

BEFORE we reach our goal, I could withstand with coolness or warmth, ease or difficulty, and being alone or with colleagues. Why do I miss saying 'I' and 'You'? I am the master of me, the leader of myself and the teacher of I. Until I leave the womb, I would call myself 'You'. 'You should never give up or bow down.' It's enough.

DAWN is coming nearer and nearer. I have been awake since midnight. I feel fresh and strong with courage. Yes. I understand that the one with inner courage dares to live, not die.

Prison in the Hands of Hitler

Saw Wai

Translated from Burmese by Ma Thida

Prison is built by men for men as a place of retribution and reform, but it became hell in Myanmar when the military staged a coup in February 2021.

For our rights to express freely, people took to the streets shouting 'no military junta'. However, our protests were crushed by force; many protestors were shot. People were dying, running, or being arrested when they couldn't run – then they were sent to interrogation camps. Some people were arrested in the daytime, then killed at night; some were arrested at night, then killed the next morning. The military junta was consolidating its power by arresting, shooting and killing, turning the country into an Auschwitz-like camp. The junta appointed persons like Adolf Eichmann to be in charge of prisons, and violated all human rights.

Young people of Generation Z, including my own daughter, support the truth, but the junta has cut off those in detention from their parents, relatives and friends, and put them in small, solitary cells. Outside those prisons, you have the parents, lovers, wives and children, who are living in a larger prison – the whole country – and the people have no chance to send even vitamins to their loved ones in jail. What is it? Is it a man-made prison? Or is this hell?

The third wave of coronavirus spreads, sent to this hell, and the junta rules people by fear. Many people die in prison, one after another. People in the wider prison, our country as a whole, pray for their kids, that they may not get on this death list; they pray to all the gods of different religions.

Let the world snatch the prisons from the military dictators and hand the country back to real human beings. The screams echo in our hearts but the junta ignores it. If the international community merely says a few words but takes no action, the junta will get strengthened even more. The junta released many criminals but arrested thousands of political prisoners. They should be released. But the junta is ignoring and rejecting all the demands – from the UN, ASEAN and all other institutions, and it is pursuing its own roadmap, which is designed to retain power. Meanwhile, many people die – prominent leaders of the opposition National League for Democracy, medical doctors and writers have all died of coronavirus; the junta stays in power.

Families don't know what is going on inside the prisons, as the junta has cut off all communication access, giving the excuse of the coronavirus outbreak. We don't know whether our kids are still alive or not, whether they are infected or not, if they are being treated properly or not.

I was charged under 505 A. The junta issued a warrant to arrest me and raided my house. I couldn't bear the idea of arrest and interrogation, I left home. My real life now is that of a poet, an ex-political prisoner who has run away from home.

As the junta is building new crematoria to manage the daily load of hundreds of dead bodies, the world must know that the junta is killing its own people.

Right now, prisons in Myanmar are in the hands of Hitler.

Belarusian Underground

Andrei Khadanovich[16]

Translated from Belarusian by Valzhyna Mort

1.

'This train doesn't stop
at the October Revolution Station,'
announces the loudspeaker.

The passengers discuss in whispers:
what's going on?
Perhaps, a breakdown at the station?
Could it be serious?

'No, it's all those revolutionaries!'
says a drunk proletarian.

A group of young people get up
and exit at the nearest stop,
the Victory Station.

2.

From the subway I call a friend.
'Are you free?' he asks.
'Yes,' I say,
'I have an hour before my lecture.'

'No,' he says. 'Are you free?'
Suddenly I get it.
'Yes, thank you!
I'm still free.'

16. Andrei Khadanovich's translation of a Polish song, *Walls*, became the most popular hymn of the Belarusian protests in 2020.

In four days, ordinary words
changed their meanings.

3.

To return to the square
after my lecture,
I could simply
cross the avenue –
and here's the square.

Yet, I take the subway,
travel for one stop,
exit
and take a few stops back by a bus.

The shortest route,
as one stalker once said,
isn't always a straight one.

4.

By the entrance to the subway
an old man is selling
warm socks.

I catch his glance
and smile
as warmly as I can.
He smiles back.

I descend into the station,
stop and look back.
The old man still follows me
with his eyes.

Visitor Hours

Notes on Exile

André Naffis-Sahely

Since no community can exist without first excluding certain groups or individuals from its ranks, the very idea of civilisation begets exile. In fact, exile has been one of our oldest and most constant companions. It begins with loss, when one is torn from one's roots and prevented from returning home, either temporarily or permanently. For some this can mean new beginnings, while for others the event becomes an insurmountable calamity, or, as Edward Said called it, the 'unhealable rift'. What does it really mean to be an exile? While the circumstances of how exile occurs can be relatively straightforward – brutality and unlawful extirpation being the primary tools in most cases – what happens after one is deracinated is often left to fate and the causality of context. Although the Ovidian conception of exile has taught us to see 'Exile' as a withered husk forever longing for the branch it was unhappily torn from, a deeper look into the field will reveal an alternative genealogy of misfits, rebels, heretics, contrarians, activists and revolutionaries. Contrary to many opinions, exile can be defiant, bold and uncompromising, examples set by Madame de Staël as she railed against Napoleon's tyranny; or the admirable stoicism worn by the communard Louise Michel on her way to the penal colony in New Caledonia; or Emma Goldman's defiance aboard the USS *Buford* as she was deported from the United States a century ago during the First Red Scare. Almost needless to say, exile can be horrifying, as the Polish legionnaires learnt while fighting to oppress a people they knew nothing about in Haiti; it can be depressing, like Giacomo Leopardi's poem on Italy's sorry state following the tumults of the Napoleonic Wars; it can speak of heroism, like the sacrifices made by the Greek poet Yannis Ritsos and the Moroccan poet Abdellatif Laâbi, both of whom spent long years in prison for their peaceful activism and their 'crimes of opinion'. Some exiles even end in triumph, the way the Russian revolutionaries of 1905 returned to rule in 1917 – a political sea-change crystallised in the image of Lenin at Finland Station. All too often, however, exile ends in tragedy, as it does for the Eritrean refugees described in Ribka Sibhatu's stirring poem, *In Lampedusa*, who died attempting to cross the

Mediterranean to begin new lives in Fortress Europe. I have always had a fondness for the eighteenth-century Venetian poet Ugo Foscolo, not that many remember him these days – which is hardly surprising. After all, Venice has never been particularly kind to its sons. It called Marco Polo a liar, it left Marcantonio Bragadin to be flayed alive in Crete, put Giacomo Casanova in irons and drove Carlo Goldoni to Paris by preferring lesser talents than his. This probably explains why there is little trace of Venice's most famous poet anywhere in that city. Born on the island of Zakynthos, Foscolo died in London, after self-exiling himself from Italy. Having witnessed the 1,200-year-old Republic meet its insurmountable end, Foscolo initially believed that Napoleon – who had entered the city proclaiming a new, egalitarian era – would help restore Venice to its former glory. Once he realised Napoleon was merely an old-fashioned conqueror in new clothes, his writings grew more critical and he was half-forced into a peripatetic way of life that he would continue to lead until his early death.

Turning to our own times, despite being one of the largest ethnic groups in the Middle East, and after close to two centuries of rampant nationalism across the world, the Kurds hold the dubious distinction of being the planet's largest stateless nation. In Kajal Ahmad's *Birds*, the author seizes upon the pain caused by this community's state of permanent exile: 'they go from country to country,' she writes, 'and still never realise their dreams of settling, /of forming a colony.' Unfortunately, whatever an exile is – and that is still up for debate – what is certain is that the future will produce many more of them. We have been banishing one another for ethnic, religious, sexual and political reasons for longer than we can remember, and sadly, as the first two decades of the twenty-first century have clearly shown us, we do not appear to have tired of these practices.

What Happens When a Writer Is Forced to Live in Exile?

Fatemeh Ekhtesari[17]

What happens when a writer is forced to live in exile?

My literary activity has faced pressure from the beginning. Iranians are passionate about art and literature, and hundreds gather in halls for weekly poetry sessions. Poetry is serious business in Iran, and the government has problems with any large gathering. The Iranian government is afraid of the influence of literature.

We would hold regular literary workshops which were routinely stopped. At the workshops, we would discuss literary criticism, philosophy and sociology.

I could not publish my books, and those that were published faced censorship and would be removed from the market, and the permission to publish would get revoked. My blog was blocked by the government. The government unleashed a campaign against Mehdi Mousavi and me – it published my private photos on national television, radio, websites and governmental news agencies, and they were trying to destroy me by calling me names and labels such as prostitute, gay, devilish, foreign spy, being vulgar and insulting saints. Since most people in Iran hate the government, it made us more popular!

In 2009, with the beginning of the Green Movement, the people's uprising against the Islamic Republic, there was a severe crackdown on the streets. The pressure on independent artists increased, particularly on poets of the postmodern ghazal, who stood by the people and defended human rights in their poems and writings, who narrated stories of people killed or imprisoned. The ghazal is an old form of poetry in Persia and many young poets write postmodern ghazals. But critics do not like how we use the language, break taboos and play games with the language. They say it weakens the poetic style.

These pressures ultimately led to the government attacking my home, seizing all my instruments and writings, arresting me and subjecting me to a long interrogation in 2010. But given that there was not much evidence against me, this interrogation ended with our being let off subject to surveillance, as well as being asked to sign a document promising not to use social media to criticise the government or face closure of our literary workshops.

Even after this, and the pressures of governmental media, the repeated summons by the government and the placing of many restrictions on us, we did not intend to leave Iran. I needed to breathe in my language, Persian, and I had to touch the pain and problems of my country closely, so that I could represent them in my art.

Women are not allowed in sport stadiums in Iran. A photo of mine was published online showing me at a stadium watching an important football match along with Mehdi Mousavi. I was dressed in men's clothing and wore make-up. We were summoned and interrogated again. Another time, I posted a simple poem on the internet about the problems of women, poverty and divorce, and it caused me to be summoned and forced to respond to the security agencies and the government. In Iran, the poetry of social problems is black washing (where the government says what you are writing portrays Iran in a bad light and causes discontent), speaking about women's problems is feminism, and feminist activity is called propaganda against the system (because the government claims that women's rights are respected in Iran, which is a lie) and saying all this may lead to the imprisonment of an artist.

Once, a singer called Shahin Najafi, who had earlier performed a number of poems of mine and Mehdi's, sang a song called *Naghi*, which, in the view of the government and religious leaders, was an insult to one of the Shia imams. They imposed a fatwa on Shahin Najafi, which, if carried out, could lead to his killing. This gave the Islamic Revolutionary Guard Corps (IRGC) an excuse to apply further pressure and we were accused of working with him.

In late 2013, the IRGC attacked my home. They seized many of my possessions and transferred me to a solitary confinement cell, blindfolded. We went through forty days of interrogations and suffered physical and mental torture. They tried to dig really deep into our writings, our emails, our photos and our diaries to find something against us. When they did not find anything, they tried to persuade me forcibly to write an admission and confession as per their words. This was sheer persecution.

International pressure as well as support from artists from Iran and elsewhere followed, and after forty days, we were freed on bail until we were to get a court sentencing. The court took about two years. During this time, I was banned from attending literary meetings or going to cultural places. The publisher who was willing to publish Mehdi Mousavi's book was murdered in suspicious circumstances. Our interrogators called us on the phone and threatened us with murder. In court, the judge, instead of hearing my defamation, reprimanded me. At the last court session, the judge read out the charges against us but did not listen to my defence or what my advocate had to say.

A few months later, I was sentenced to eleven and a half years' imprisonment and ninety-nine lashes and Mehdi Mousavi to nine years' imprisonment and ninety-nine lashes. This sentence was confirmed in the Appeals Court later. The main charge against us was the text of our lyrics, which dealt with freedom, minority rights, the raising of society's problems, expressing taboos, women's rights, and criticising traditions. The other reasons given included holding literary workshops, collaborating with underground singers, communicating with human rights organisations and reading poetry abroad. The lashes were for shaking hands with a person of the opposite sex, although shaking hands is quite common among most people in Iran. They also destroyed all our poems, stories, films and manuscripts, so we have no copies of many of them today.

After the verdict, given its length and given the certainty that I would not have security even after my prison term was finished, I decided to leave Iran. I am known in Iran, and our homes and our phones were monitored by the government. I applied make-up to my face and ran away illegally. I had many problems along the way. I arrived in Iraqi Kurdistan. I was hiding there for a while, but due to the influence of the IRGC in Iraq, I had to flee again. I went to Turkey with support from Kurdish smugglers.

Eventually I arrived in Turkey and introduced myself to the UN Refugee Office. I had to change my city, and in the end, with the help of the International Cities of Refuge Network (ICORN), I was issued a temporary passport and visa and was transferred to Norway.

I am safe now, but a writer's main tool is language, and I miss my language.

Rohingya Writers Living 'In the Jail of Fresh Air'

James Byrne

In 2019, I visited Cox's Bazar refugee camp in Bangladesh to facilitate the first-ever creative writing workshops in the camps with Rohingya refugees. Along with my co-editor Shehzar Doja, I worked with young Rohingya poets and folk singers, and subsequently a book, *I am a Rohingya: Poems from the Camps and Beyond,* was published. Though frequently innovative, many of the poems read like testimonies or witness accounts, documenting systematic killings, rape and torture of the Rohingya people.[18] There are also poems relating to daily confinement or imprisonment. Ro B.M. Hairu sees his homeland of Arakan as being 'turned into a central jail'. Zaki Ovais writes that he is 'a dove on the street of Yangon, / jailed in the cage of inhumanity'. Yasmin Ullah's long poem *Birth* declares that 'if there's a chance, [to] walk out of prison, / free, / they are still imprisoned / by the vicious cycle of being / Rohingya.'[19]

Since the military coup in Myanmar in early 2021, figures for detained or imprisoned Rohingya are hard to obtain. The fight to live in conditions where basic human rights are respected for this ethnic minority – still one of the most persecuted people in a world of humanitarian crises – is very much an ongoing struggle. Tellingly, whilst the world turns its attention elsewhere, the COVID pandemic has seen an increase in violence against the Rohingya.[20] Several arson attacks on the camp have claimed lives (who would want to torch the homes of people already displaced?). The refugee camp at Cox's Bazar, which is the largest in the world, is in fact spread over twenty camps, all precariously flammable because of an intense, dry heat. The tents are cramped, housing generations of families. Often husbands and young men are conspicuously absent, killed in Myanmar. I met a lot of children who are orphans.

18. The anthology was presented as supplementary evidence at the Hague trial attended by Aung San Suu Kyi in 2019.

19. Published in *I am a Rohingya: Poems from the Camps and Beyond* (Arc Publications, 2019).

20. Initial media sources in Rakhine State suggested that the Rohingya would not be given a COVID-19 vaccine, until a channel called 'Western News' just this week said the Chinese Sinovac vaccine would be made available. This is the same vaccine being given out to Rohingya refugees in the camps.

During the pandemic, many NGOs have had to lessen their support or withdraw from Cox's Bazar entirely. Furthering their traumatic experience, 20,000 Rohingya have been transferred to Bhasan Char, a remote, floodable island which has consistently been referred to as a prison, replete with watchtowers and living arrangements reminiscent of a concentration camp.[21] Bangladesh is celebrating fifty years of independence in 2021, having itself survived a brutal history. But it has, like the Burmese military (the Tatmadaw), blood on its hands. During the recent monsoon, eight Rohingya died in Bhasan Char because of flooding.

I remain in touch with several writers from the workshop, those living inside and outside the camp. If given the basic chance of an education (denied in Arakan by the Burmese government and now in the camps by the Bangladeshi authorities), they would *still* struggle. For example, the only existing educational scholarship program specifically designed for the Rohingya is in Turkey. On the surface, it would seem to be a lifeline for any Rohingya student – a chance to escape the camps for a university degree. And yet, neither the Bangladeshi nor the Turkish government offers support for relocation, visas, passports, etc. The only option left to those accepted is to try and be smuggled out of the country, sacrificing hundreds of dollars (and, of course, their own safety) at the hands of a 'broker'. What kind of *opportunity* is this? Often, prospective students can't even board a plane. A broader system of imprisonment is at work for a new generation of Rohingya, as it was for their parents in Myanmar.

So, how do you get an education if you're Rohingya? Inside the camps, refugees themselves are setting up their own educational initiatives which are impressive, extending to the vital (but often neglected) task of offering education for women. However, funds are limited and both the Bangladeshi and Myanmar governments frequently create oppositional roadblocks. It is still illegal to set up a school of any kind in the camps.

A few writers I know of have risked everything to get out of the camps and find education in Bangladesh. To do this, you have to obtain false documents (again, exploited by a broker), find a university that will take you in, and

21. https://www.hrw.org/news/2021/06/07/bangladeshs-unplanned-relocation-rohingya-refugees-bhasan-char-island-risky.

(this must be the worst part) change your identity, hoping every day that nobody will recognise you as being Rohingya. Some students have been arrested and sent back to Myanmar, others are itinerant, frequently moving from accommodation to accommodation, wary of snitchers. And these are perhaps the lucky ones, in the sense that they are literate, able to pay the endless bribes and somehow live outside the camp.

What is the future for the Rohingya, living as they do in various kinds of imprisonment? Almost a million live in Cox's Bazar or Bhasan Char, others are still in Myanmar. Whether inside or outside the camp, the Rohingya remain systematically oppressed. Just this week, a camp leader told Rohingya elders they were not to hold any gatherings to commemorate the fourth year of the genocide. This is shocking even by recent Bangladeshi government standards.

Ultimately, there is no excuse for this continued treatment of the Rohingya people. How can it be, as Pacifist Farooq has written, that anyone can live as 'a prisoner in the jail of fresh air'?

James Byrne, 26 August 2021

Thanks to Ro and Farooq, to whom this piece is dedicated.

Tower of broken pencil points

Regret, My Friend, Is Our Closest Enemy

Ali Cobby Eckermann

Poetry in Australia is thriving. Aboriginal poetry in Australia is thriving and surviving. Surviving the past 230 years of colonisation is testament to the original people of the land who have survived the imprisonment of their sacred lands. These lands form a beautiful, varied and vast continent. The continent is an island. Prison Island.

This island is my spiritual home. The prison has been built in my mind. My incarceration began at birth when I was tricked away from my mother and family, like thousands of other Aboriginal children born since colonisation. My birthplace was an out-of-sight adoption agency in a seaside suburb along the urban coast of Adelaide in South Australia, where I resided for a couple of months. Four months later, in a suburban courthouse, I was adopted into a German Lutheran family. New name. New parents. New family. New freedoms.

As a First Nations woman, I see freedom as often mislabelled. The reality of freedom is often shattered by the reality of re-incarceration. The reality in Australia is that most children removed from their families are sexually abused by the new society that spouts to adopt their care. My resistance of such abuse resulted in a farm accident in which I was run over and my femur broken, requiring two months of traction and a half-body plaster cast. Incarceration continued in the children's hospital. A nurse cut off my beautiful ponytail without my parents' consent and the adjunct schoolteacher loudly belittled me as I lay in the ward with my broken leg suspended by weights from the apparatus above me because I got distracted by the excitement of learning to weave a small cane basket. I was eight years old.

By the time I was discharged from the hospital for home detention, I had transformed into a replica of my mugshot. My heart no longer reflected a happy and energetic child. I had been registered on the Prisoners list. After this realisation, I sought the sanctuary of reading. The justice I sought in my innocence of place and righteousness was through the curiosity of stories. School was a nightmare I absorbed and detested in equal measure. At seventeen, I saw a chance of escape and ran away.

The continent is an island. Prison Island. I could not escape despite changing every detail of my habitation inside the new landscape. I had run to live along the Indian Pacific railway line in one of the remotest areas of the desert country in South Australia, at Ooldea. It was shocking to realise the prison extended here. Within weeks I was brutalised by domestic violence by the person who had helped me to escape. He was paid every fortnight; I received blackened eyes. One's spirit can almost retire in the most dreadful situations. One's spirit can also revive. A prison break, and I was free to return to my upbringing, returned to prison garb at the discovery of my pregnancy. I was deemed incapable of caring for my firstborn child. Prison guards were everywhere and there was no escape from this relinquishment. Now there is little distinction between my mugshot and my physical self. The prison had entered my mind.

Over many years, I carried the prison internally whilst wandering across the beautiful, varied and vast continent, seeking any form of respite and retribution. A life at risk. Alcoholism. A motorbike accident resulting in disability. Drug addiction. A stillborn child. A failed marriage. Rehabilitation. The Twelve Steps. Finding my mother. Aboriginal Art school. Finding my son. Aboriginal Adult education. No longer do I wear the mugshot on my face. No longer is the prison inside of me. I have reclaimed my mind and am articulating my journey with poetry. Aboriginal poetry in Australia is thriving and surviving. Surviving the past 230 years of colonisation is testament to the original people of the land who have survived the imprisonment of their sacred lands. Many people deny that Australia suffers an underlying current of racism towards its native people. Read our poetry. Know our truth. The continent is an island. Prison Island.

Nieces and Nephews

Marilyn Hacker

And because the rain
Has come to live on a hill in the suburbs…
Sa'adi Yussef: A Fleeting Hallucination

In July, when Tsahal was bombing Gaza
and we marched, and there were flags and brawls
Lamis waited for me on the corner, smiling
in a lime-green sleeveless dress, not her daily jeans.
There were three cop cars parked in front of my building
and Lamis shouted giddily in Arabic
'She's the terrorist, here!' I pinched her,
shushed her, laughing 'Half those cops are Arabs!'
We went to a café, drank wine. She told me
her niece had finally been freed from prison
in Damascus. She lit up her cell phone
to show me the 19-year-old girl's photo.
The second of her older sister's children.

Naima's Ismaël on the Corniche, sunlit
in a rust corduroy jacket, white shirt open
at the neck, smiles next to his aunt in paisley
hijab and movie-star dark glasses.
Wind scuds the waves beyond. Out of Mosul
for the first time in his life, she, out of danger
for the first time in six months. The last
check-point, the last baksheesh, the abaya
shoved into a suitcase. A walk on Sunday,
a future open as the wine-dark sea.

I drank wine in the same café with Fadwa
last week, at midnight, talking about meters –

blank verse, alexandrines and al-mursal –
though she was keen to go outside and smoke
in the insidious slant winter rain.
'Have you heard from Lamis? I haven't seen her
in a month, she didn't answer an e-mail.'
'Her nephew,' said Fadwa, 'died in prison.
He was tortured.' The first of those five children.

I'll meet Ismaël in Beirut with Naima.
In Beirut, no one arrests the daughters
or the nephews of the neighbors these days,
so she can bitch and moan about the neighbors
and how her students can't translate as-Sayyab's
'Nothing but Iraq…' The rain is falling
on all the suburbs where it lives in exile
and Lamis isn't answering the phone.

Extracts from a Conversation with Malay Roychoudhury

Kandivali, Mumbai, 2018

Shilpa Gupta

Malay Roychoudhury was part of a movement in Bengali poetry that came to be known as the Hungryalists. It was started in the 1960s and included Shakti Chattopadhyaya, Samir Roychowdhury, Haradhan Dhara (Debi Roy) and others. The Hungryalists challenged contemporary ideas of aesthetics and society and sought to provoke their readers. In 1965, Roychoudhury was charged and jailed for a month by the West Bengal government on obscenity charges, leading to a three-year ordeal for the poet. In 2018, Shilpa Gupta spoke to him about his experiences, as part of her research for the sound installation, 'For, In Your Tongue, I Cannot Fit'.

*

We started a literary culture movement in 1961 by publishing a manifesto on poetry. It was called the Hungry Generation. At that time, I was residing in Patna, where I studied and where my parents were living. We wanted to start the movement in Bengali literature. However there was no Bengali press in Patna, so I got the manifesto printed in English – which was better because it reached various states. (In Bengali, it would have been circulated only in Calcutta.[22]) That was in November 1961.

Then people came to know about the movement and young writers and students started joining it. Gradually, newspapers started writing about us and started printing our manifestos. When we started publishing in Bengali, some of the Bengali newspapers wrote editorials also.

Subimal Basak drew a lot of explicit pictures which enraged the elites of Calcutta. Earlier, in the nineteenth century or early twentieth century, only

22. Patna is the capital of Bihar, a Hindi-speaking state that neighbours West Bengal, where Bengali (the poet's native language) is spoken.

upper-class people ruled over the the values of art as such. Art did not belong to lower -caste people. It was meant only for the higher class, who understood only Greek or Roman ideas of art, because when the British came here, they introduced the concepts of art or art for art's sake. Art not for people's sake. So, we (published writers from the lower class) started attacking these (higher class) people – academicians – in various ways. We inverted everything. We had poetry readings in Khalasi Tola (country liquor shop) – the cheapest one in Calcutta – at poet Michael Madhusudan Dutt's tomb and at a burning ghat.[23] Can you imagine a love poem being read in a burning ghat? These things enraged the establishment.

Once, we purchased and distributed about hundred wedding cards on which was written 'Fuck the Bastards of Gangshalik School of Poetry'. There was no such Gangshalik school. Shalik means a mynah, a bird, as most of them were using birds, stars, trees and butterflies in their poems. We then sent cheap cardboard masks of *Rakshash* and animals – on the flip side, we got printed, 'Please take off your mask – from Hungry Generation, with regards'. They got very angry. (The masks were) sent to the Police commissioner, the chief minister, district magistrates of districts neighboring Calcutta, academicians, reporters, chief reporters and editors.

People started complaining to the police and some of the broadsheets started printing front-page news like 'Right in front of the Calcutta Police commissioner's nose, these ruffians are writing obscene things. They do not know how to write. They are spoiling the language', et cetera. The Police Commissioner became enraged, or he was pushed into a corner. In September 1964, arrest warrants were issued against eleven of us, because in one issue ten persons had written and my elder brother[24] was the publisher. Later, I came to know that they thought I was the guru of the entire thing, and I must be punished. So, other than section 292 for obscenity, they also charged (me) under 120 B for conspiracy.[25] If 120 B is charged, then it becomes a non-

23. A platform at the top of a riverside ghat, used for the cremation of the dead.
24. He was a classmate and contemporary of Bengali writers Sunil Gangopadhyaya and Shakti Chattopadhyaya.
25. Section 120(B) makes it a punishable offence to be part of a criminal conspiracy for a crime whose punishment exceeds two years (up to the death penalty) as if the person has abetted the crime. Section 292 deals with obscenity, where a book, pamphlet, paper, writing, drawing, painting, or any representation of a figure or an object is deemed to be obscene if it is lascivious, or appeals to the prurient interest, or if its effect may deprave or corrupt the person exposed to it.

bailable offence. I was handcuffed, a rope tied around me, and I had to walk with the policeman up to the thana (station).

*

I was working in the Reserve Bank (of India) at that time. Since my handwriting was good, my job was to write names on bonds using calligraphy. The police had come to my office, but they didn't tell the chief of my office why exactly, saying that we have some work and so we want to talk to him downstairs. They were in mufti (plainclothes), not in police uniform. When I went down, they caught hold of me and called a (cycle) rickshaw, and went to my house. There they searched all the rooms. They even opened my mother's tin trunk with an iron rod and her wedding Banarasi saris tore. They collected some twenty-one items – my typewriter, books, everything. Even some unnecessary books – from the title itself someone could say that it is a literary work and not something obscene or against the State.

*

I was arrested and put in the lockup. The lockup was quite dark, very dark, there was no light. It was night-time, but I could sense from the voices that there were several people inside. Someone saw me against the window and said, 'Sir, there is a fellow, he is quite drunk, and people are urinating in that corner. So, what we have done, we have stopped the flow of urine with this man.' This drunkard was there as a bank. In the morning, when I had to go to the toilet, the policeman tied a rope, and told me to go and do it, and then come back. After I came back, he told me, 'What type of idiot you are. You could have just untied and ran away. Your case is only for writing. Who bothers about writing? These fellows in the lockup, they are dacoits, there is one murderer, there is one pickpocket and you have just written something. The police would have forgotten all these things. Why did you come back?'

The next day, we went to the local Patna court, all seven of us. We were tied with ropes because at that time it was the rule. I know that apart from us, some six or seven who were arrested, some people were also invited to be prosecution witness against us. A chargesheet was filed against me only because I was the leader. At that time, I came to know that some poets had become police witness against me and some of those arrested, two of them, became approvers against me, making the case watertight for the police.

The police also had two false witnesses, including a friend of mine who was in the movement. So that they could get free and cases were not framed against them.

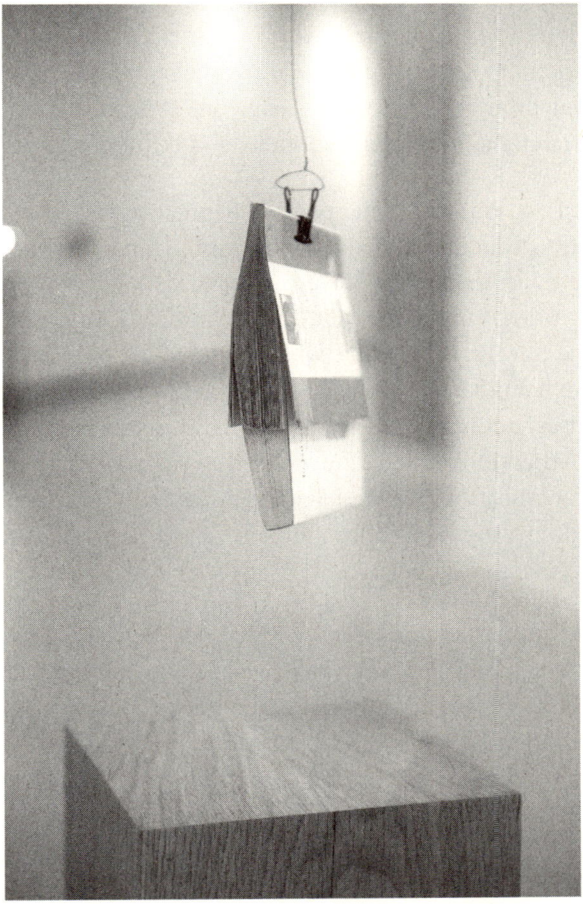

Two interlocked books

In conversation with Sara Hossain

Salil Tripathi

The conversations at our home had always been about issues of justice. We witnessed different incidents and saw people speaking up and trying to act on their convictions. So, what gets me up in the morning is that it is almost inevitable, you know you have to act – someone is taking action, someone is asking you to join them or requiring some kind of support.

We expect writers, journalists and poets to be the conscience of society, who provoke us into thinking and not living a mundane existence, accepting everything around us. In our society, journalists play an enormous role because the press is probably the only institution that still has some independence to call out injustice when they see it. Some do get captured – they end up being servants of the State or get close to the officialdom, or powers-that-be – but many still aren't, and because they aren't, they are not being strangled, and their not being silenced is critical. That's why when they face attacks, or when they are subjected to litigation or harassment through cases, through investigations, through prosecution, it is really important to step up and speak for them.

They see the things that no one else will see, no one else will dare to speak about. They don't provoke only for its own sake, but they challenge the constraints imposed by reality and social morality. They defy convention and force us to think. It isn't the officialdom alone that tries to stop them, but also social constraints, extremists, and others who deny space, who prevent us from trying to lead free lives and think freely. Poets and writers make us question ourselves and that's why they often cross the lines.

The most recent case I worked on involved the photo journalist, writer and occasional poet Shahidul Alam. He faced prosecution for an offence, now repealed, under the Information Communications and Technology Act. He was accused in relation to a Facebook post and the alleged content of an interview that he gave to Al Jazeera. That case was important because he was a symbol of not only the media, but also of the civil society speaking about a completely taboo subject – the challenges to having free and fair elections. Not only did he speak about it, but he spoke to the international media, which was seen as washing dirty linen in public.

He was a really important symbolic target for the government, which wanted to silence everyone who might have otherwise thought of speaking up. It was incredibly effective because, in the whole country, many of those who would have spoken fell silent after what happened. But his case was important for another reason too, for how people mobilised around it – his immediate colleagues, family and friends mounted quite an incredible campaign, expressing solidarity, being continuously present in front of the prison, in the courtroom, in the press, on the streets, through protests, and online, communicating with a whole network of people who knew him and some who didn't know him and wanted to support this case, to ensure his freedom. That case was emblematic about what you can do and what you have to do when such situations occur. Ultimately, he secured bail from the high court, but has still not had any redress for torture or ill-treatment, and the police are still investigating the case.

Shahidul himself is a very well-known figure nationally and internationally, and much more so after the case than before. So, it was counter-productive for those who chose to prosecute him, and as it happens in these cases, they ended up amplifying his voice much more than could have happened otherwise.

There was another case some years ago, of Arifur Rahman, a young cartoonist who was from a village but came into the national spotlight because he won the first prize at a competition run by Transparency International on the subject of corruption. He got a job with *Prothom Alo* (First Light), the leading newspaper in our country. It ran a cartoon by him in its magazine, about the Prophet and a cat. This led to the most extraordinary reaction.

The timing was very important. The country was in a state of emergency and the military were effectively in power and there was a strange alliance with fundamentalist groups. Arif faced death threats, there were processions insisting that he be immediately prosecuted and jailed, and he was accused of hurting religious sentiments. The case was brought by a police officer. Arif was held in prison with some of the people who had actually been threatening him. He was violently assaulted in prison. (Shahidul too stated before a court that he was tortured while he was in police custody.) Arif came out ultimately because the person who had originally brought the complaint didn't pursue it. But Arif could not remain in the country, even though he was very talented. Whoever gave him work subsequently said that they weren't willing to let him use his name because they didn't want the risk, even though his name is extremely common. So, he unfortunately ended up going abroad. His voice too has been amplified. He has continued to make cartoons and initiate competitions.

Then there is the case of Tanvir Mokammel, who is a well-known filmmaker and also an activist. The first film of his that we had to defend against the censors was *Nodir Naam Modhumoti* (A River Named Madhumati,1996), which dealt with Islamic fundamentalism. The censors did not like a scene where someone lit a cigarette during azan (prayer) and they insisted that it be cut. In another scene, Tanvir was trying to critique the ritualism of qurbani (sacrifice) and he showed that in some gory detail. That scene was cut. We defended him. In the end, we won and the film was released. There was another film, a documentary called *Karnaphulir Kanna*, about the Chittagong Hill Tracts and the military's role. Again, cuts were proposed and again we challenged those decisions of the censors in the Supreme Court, and got orders, and he was able to release the film.

The oldest and the earliest significant free expression case I worked on was about the well-known poet and writer Taslima Nasreen. She faced a number of different cases, but the big one which led her to go into hiding was not because of any literary writing but an interview that she had given to the *Statesman* of Kolkata. A statement was ascribed to her where she supposedly said that there could be some revisions to the Koran. She said she hadn't actually said that, and I had not heard any recording or seen notes, and the newspaper wasn't even available in Bangladesh. This was in the pre-internet days, so you could have read it only if someone carried it across the border. But the headlines were republished in Bangladeshi newspapers, in particular the fundamentalist newspapers, and some headlines were in red, and pre-internet trolling started: group statements by university professors and doctors, engineers and others, denouncing her, and again calling for action against her. There were processions and demonstrations. A case was filed for hurting religious sentiments and she had to pretty much go underground for weeks. Shahidul actually hid her to protect her for some time, and who knew then, that twenty–thirty years later, he would be in a similar situation?

These cases are not meant to imprison you, but to harass you into silence. At that time, unfortunately, there were some famous people who spoke critically against her, including feminists, who asked why did she have to say such things; how she has put everyone in a difficult situation by speaking out. But there were honourable exceptions who supported her.

She had to be brought to the court to seek bail. While we haven't had situations in Pakistan where the accused in blasphemy cases were killed on court premises, we feared that something like that might happen. There was lobbying behind the scenes and attempts to explain to the government how extremely negative the entire action against Taslima was proving to be for them. At that time, we didn't have the offence of hurting the image of the nation. If we had, we could have said to the government that you are hurting the image of the nation by prosecuting her. Some people in the government saw the point. The attorney general felt the case was absurd and he didn't oppose her getting bail. He discussed it with the defence counsel, who included my father and other senior lawyers, whom I was assisting.

There's a real distinction to be made between *offence* and *harm*. If there is a risk of harm, such that you're inciting violence against particular individuals or communities, then clearly the criminal law has to step in. But in other instances such as defamation, there should only be civil action, for seeking damages. Using the criminal law is completely unconscionable in these cases.

If you find any content offensive, why read it? You don't need to be offended. You have to go out of your way to be offended, you have to pick up those articles and read them. It is not like they are on every billboard in front of you, being rammed down your throat.

Now people are going out of their way to be offended and that's one consequence of being surrounded by information. If you choose to be offended and go out of your way to seek offence and then attack the speaker, then no one will feel free to speak any longer.

People do have the right to offend, and offence is in some cases necessary.

Provocative challenge is necessary to make people think afresh, if we don't want to live in a stagnant society where we just doff our caps all the time. The offended definitely have the right to speak and to be heard, and the right to write back and respond and speak and argue, but not to do any more than that.

There are some regrets – there was one case that I wasn't able to work on and it is really a source of quite considerable shame to me that I didn't work on it. It was a particular case on contempt of court faced by a very good journalist friend who died due to COVID – Mizanur Rahman Khan. He was an extraordinary legal scholar as well as writer.

I haven't personally faced threats from fundamentalists, although there have been threats from State officials and security agencies under different governments. A lot of what I decide to do, or not do, is my decision. But Mizan's was one case where I saw how commercial reality can affect our professional decisions.

These kinds of pressures are increasing in our society. You take up cases because you believe in them, and then you can see certain kinds of work won't come your way, such as corporate work, because some companies will be frightened off by the government pressure. And yet, despite all these constraints, we still have that little bit of space in our judiciary and in the media where people are willing to speak and amplify issues. That's what makes it possible to keep going. There are groups and individuals who do come together: Why do they do what they do? They are standing up on issues; they don't sit and accept, they aren't speaking only about the rising gross domestic product and growth. Though we all take pride in that, some also want to see why everything is not as it should be.

Knowing that there are colleagues and comrades around is a great source of support.

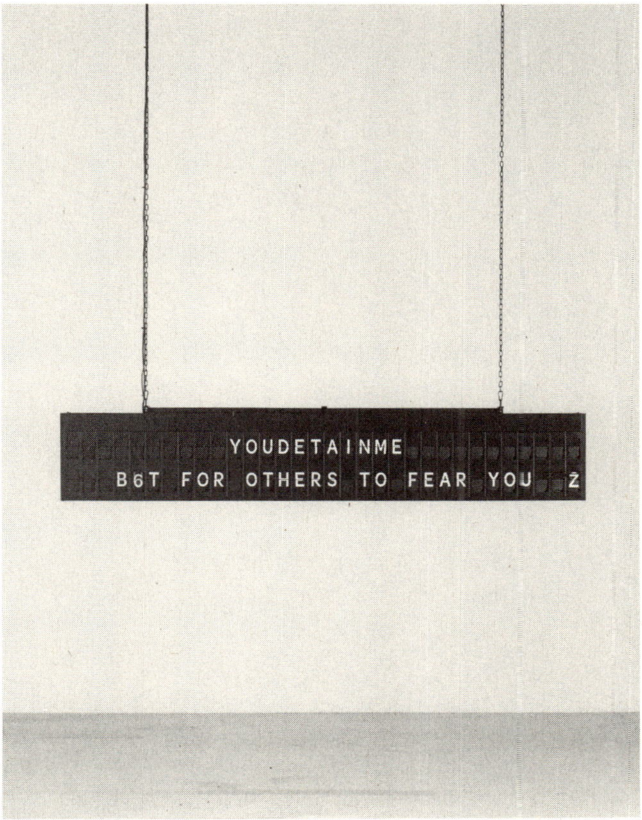

Words Come From Ears

Note from Dallas Contemporary

Emily Edwards

Shilpa Gupta's multichannel immersive sound installation 'For, In Your Tongue, I Cannot Fit' is the outcome of a years-long research project into persecuted poets across time and geographies. The physical installation spans over 3,000 square feet and includes 100 microphones suspended from the ceiling. They play an audio loop of snippets of poems whose authors have been subjected to imprisonment, detainment and execution. The poems are dated from the eighth century to contemporary times and are read in languages including English, Spanish, Arabic, Russian, Azeri and Hindi, allowing visitors to experience over a thousand years of global poetry in an hour. With this work, Gupta gives the microphone back to those who were rendered voiceless.

For over two decades, the Mumbai-based artist has explored incorporating elements of sound into her work to expand the parameters of what art can be. One of her leitmotifs is a reverse-wired microphone that operates as a speaker. Having first utilised this mechanism in her 2008 work, 'In Our Times', Gupta has repeatedly returned to it since. Her sound installations require her viewers to actively listen, allowing the artist to engage more directly with her audience on critical topics such as borders, diversity, inclusion and the freedom of speech. This installation serves as an invitation to visitors to listen and respond, completing the work's meaning. Unlike most participatory art, rather than the viewer changing the artwork, the goal is for the artwork to change the viewer.

When Gupta and I first discussed exhibiting her sound installation at Dallas Contemporary, she shared that her full vision included a publication that would coincide with the audio element, so the poems featured would have a chance to be experienced past the physical exhibition. This work includes sixty of the poems included in the sound piece, as well as additional commissioned poems, essays and short texts, photographs and existing and new drawings by the artist. The poems on display are words that have survived despite censorship and oppression, and this book assists in giving them another life.

This publication has been made possible with the generous grant by the National Endowment for the Arts, the years of dedication by artist Shilpa Gupta, the enduring support of Salil Tripathi, the former chair of PEN International's Writers in Prison Committee, the assistance of Shilpa's studio team, Czetan Patil, Pooja Tilve and Pranav Gogwekar, as well as Tina Marie Monelyon.

We are most grateful to the artist, Shilpa Gupta, for granting us the privilege to host her moving installation and to support this publication.

Voltaire

Contributors

ALI COBBY ECKERMANN

Ali Cobby Eckermann's first poetry collection *Little Bit Long Time* was published in 2009. In 2013, she received the Kenneth Slessor Poetry Prize and Book Of The Year (in the NSW Premier's Awards) for *Ruby Moonlight*. Ali is the first Aboriginal Australian writer to attend the International Writing Program in Iowa, USA, and received a Windham Campbell Award from Yale University in 2017. She was awarded a literature fellowship by the Australian Council for the Arts in 2018. She is currently an adjunct professor at Royal Melbourne Institute of Technology.

ANDRÉ NAFFIS-SAHELY

André Naffis-Sahely is the author of *The Promised Land: Poems from Itinerant Life* (Penguin, 2017) and the editor of *The Heart of a Stranger: An Anthology of Exile Literature* (Pushkin Press, 2020). His second collection, *High Desert*, will be published by Bloodaxe Books in 2022.

ANDREI KHADANOVICH

Andrei Khadanovich is a Belarusian poet and translator. He is the author of thirteen books of poetry and twenty-nine books of translation into Belarusian. A recipient of the Crystal of Vilenica Award in Slovenia and the Zbigniew Dominyaka Prize in Poland, Khadanovich has been honoured with a plethora of awards in Belarus, including the Book of the Year in 2015. His translation of the Polish song *Walls* became the most popular hymn of the Belarusian protests in 2020.

BURHAN SONMEZ

Burhan Sonmez is the president of PEN International, elected at the Centennial Congress in September 2021. He is the author of five novels, which have been translated into forty-two languages. He was born in Turkey and grew up speaking Turkish and Kurdish. He worked as a lawyer in Istanbul before going to Britain as a political exile. His writing has appeared in *The Guardian*, *Der Spiegel* and *La Repubblica*. He has translated William Blake's *The Marriage of Heaven and Hell* into Turkish. Burhan has previously been a lecturer in literature at the Middle East Technical University, Turkey. He received the Vaclav Havel Library Award in 2017 and the EBRD Literature Prize in 2018. Burhan holds dual Turkish and British citizenship. He lives between Istanbul and Cambridge.

DAREEN TATOUR

Dareen Tatour is a Palestinian poet, photographer, political and social media activist. Her debut poetry collection, *The Last Invasion (or War)*, was published in 2010. In 2018, she was tried and convicted in an Israeli occupation court for inciting violence and supporting a terrorist organisation, following the publication of her poem *Resist My People, Resist Them* on social media. She was released in 2018 after serving a prison term. Dareen is the recipient of the OXFAM Novib/PEN award 2019 for Freedom of Expression. A Hebrew online magazine, *Maayan*, awarded Tatour the 2016 prize for 'Creativity in Struggle', and she was also awarded the Danish Carl Scharenberg Prize for standing against injustice through her poetry in 2017. In 2020, she won the Freedom of Expression Award, Norway.

DEVANGANA KALITA

Devangana Kalita is a feminist activist associated with Pinjra Tod (Break the Cage), a women students' collective in India. She is a currently a research scholar at Jawaharlal Nehru University (JNU), New Delhi, and her work focuses on gender, memory and labour history. She has graduated from Delhi University and the Institute of Development Studies, UK. Devangana was arrested in May 2020 and imprisoned for thirteen months by the Indian State, charged under a draconian anti-terror law for her participation in the protests that demanded the repeal of the discriminatory Citizenship Amendment Act (CAA).

EMILY EDWARDS

Emily Edwards is the assistant curator at Dallas Contemporary. Prior to Dallas, she worked at the 9/11 Memorial Museum, the Barnes Foundation, the Hirshhorn Museum and Sculpture Garden, and the Isabella Stewart Gardner Museum. Her research interests include memorialisation, diasporic art and social commentary. She graduated with a BFA with honours in art history from the University of Texas at Austin and an MA in art history and museum studies from Georgetown University.

FATEMEH EKHTESARI

Fatemeh Ekhtesari is an Iranian poet and writer and is editor in chief for a Persian literary magazine. She has published five poetry collections, two short-story collections and two poly-genre books. In 2013, she was imprisoned and later released on bail. The verdict on her case came in 2015, sentencing her to ninety-nine lashes and 11.5 years imprisonment for crimes against the Iranian regime and blasphemy. She is a FreeCity Writer from ICORN and lives in Norway now.

GAUTAM BHATIA

Gautam Bhatia is an Indian constitutional lawyer and science fiction writer. He is the author of the legal texts, *Offend, Shock or Disturb* and *The Transformative Constitution*, and of the science fiction duology, *The Wall* and *The Horizon*.

GOPIKA JADEJA

Gopika Jadeja is a bilingual poet and translator from India, writing in English and Gujarati. Her current literary project deals with archives and de-centring and challenging colonial epistemologies. She has also been working on a project of English translations of poetry from Gujarat. Her literary writing and translations have been published widely. She currently lives and works in Singapore.

IAN PROBSTEIN

Ian Probstein is a professor of English at Touro College, and a bilingual Russian-American poet, scholar and translator of poetry. He has published two books of literary criticism, twelve books of poetry in Russian, one in English, translated more than a dozen poetry volumes, and has compiled and edited more than thirty books and anthologies of poetry in translation, apart from several other publications to his name. His essays, poems in English and translations of poetry into English have been published in journals such as *Atlantic Review*, *The International Literary Quarterly* and *Brooklyn Rail*.

JACK COX

Jack Cox is an independent translator based in France.

JAMES BYRNE

James Byrne is a poet, editor, translator and visual artist. His most recent collection is *Places you Leave* (Arc Publications, 2022).

JENNIFER CLEMENT

Jennifer Clement is president emerita of PEN International and the only woman to hold the office of president (2015–2021) since the organisation was founded in 1921. Clement is the author of the award-winning novels *A True Story Based on Lies*, *The Poison that Fascinates*, *Prayers for the Stolen* and *Gun Love*, as well as several poetry books. Clement has also written the acclaimed memoir *Widow Basquiat*, on New York City in the early 1980s and the painter Jean-Michel Basquiat. Her books have been translated into more than thirty-five languages. *Prayers for the Stolen* has been made into a movie directed by Tatiana Huezo and is Mexico's Oscar selection for 2022.

KARTHIKA NAÏR

Poet, fabulist and librettist, Karthika Naïr is the author of several books, including the award-winning *Until the Lions: Echoes from the Mahabharata*. Her latest is *A Different Distance: A Renga* (Milkweed Editions, 2021), written with American poet Marilyn Hacker. The performances she has scripted and co-scripted have been staged at venues across the world, such as Palais des Papes (Avignon), Esplanade (Singapore) and Lincoln Center (New York). Also a dance enabler, Naïr's closest association has been with Sidi Larbi Cherkaoui and Damien Jalet as executive producer of works like *Babel (Words)*, *Puz/zle and Les Médusés*, and as co-founder of Cherkaoui's Antwerp-based company, Eastman.

KHALED MATTAWA

Khaled Mattawa was born and grew up in Benghazi, Libya, and moved to the US in 1979. He teaches at the University of Michigan, where he also edits the *Michigan Quarterly Review*. Mattawa's poetry is about migration, memory and displacement. His poetry collections include *Fugitive Atlas* (2020), *Tocqueville* (2010), *Amorisco* (2008), *Zodiac of Echoes* (2003), and *Ismailia Eclipse* (1995). He has published a critical study of Mahmoud Darwish, and translated Adonis, Saadi Youssef and Iman Mersal, among many other Arab poets. He is the recipient of many honours, including the Guggenheim Fellowship, several Pushcart Prizes, the PEN Award for Literary Translation, and the MacArthur Fellowship.

LAUREN PYOTT

Lauren Pyott is a freelance translator, editor, researcher and writer based in the Scottish Highlands. She translates literary texts from Arabic to English and has coordinated a number of poetry translation workshops between poets based in Scotland and the Middle East. She has edited several literary anthologies, including the trilingual poetry collection *This Room is Waiting: Poems from Iraq and Scotland* (Freight Books, 2014). Her research looks at the politics of solidarity in the cultural industry, and she writes about internationalist perspectives from the north of Scotland.

MA THIDA

Ma Thida is a medical doctor, writer, human rights activist and former prisoner of conscience. She edits the magazine *Shwe Amyutay*, the journal *Info Digest*, and also volunteers at a local free clinic. In 1993, she was sentenced to twenty years in prison for 'endangering public peace, having contact with illegal organizations, and distributing unlawful literature'. She was released in 1999 due to declining health and increasing political pressure from efforts of organisations like Amnesty International and PEN International. She has won several international human rights awards, including the Reebok Human Rights Award, the PEN/Barbara Goldsmith Freedom to Write Award, Freedom of Speech Award and Disturbing the Peace; Courageous Writer at Risk Award. She was an International Writers Project Fellow at Brown University and a fellow of the Radcliffe Institute for Advanced Studies at Harvard University. She was the inaugural elected president of PEN Myanmar, and has served as a board member of PEN International from 2016 to 2021. She was elected as the chair of Writers in Prison Committee of PEN International in 2021 and is currently working as a visiting scholar with the Southeast Asia Studies Department at Yale University.

MALAY ROYCHOUDHURY

Malay Roychoudhury is an Indian poet, playwright, essayist and novelist who founded the Hungryalist movement in Bengali literature. Roychoudhury introduced confessional poetry to Bengali literature with his 1963 poem, *Stark Electric Jesus* (Prachanda Baidyutik Chhutar). The poem defied traditional forms as well as meters. He was arrested for the poem and the trial went on for thirty-five months. Later, he was exonerated by the high court. Till date, Roychoudhury has written more than 200 works of fiction, poetry, translations, drama and essays. He lives with his wife in Mumbai.

MARILYN HACKER

Marilyn Hacker is the author of fourteen books of poetry, including *A Stranger's Mirror* (Norton, 2015) and *Blazons* (Carcanet, 2019), two collaborative books, *Diaspo/Renga* (Holland Park Press, 2014) written with Deema K. Shehabi and *A Different Distance* (Milkweed Editions, 2021) written with Karthika Naïr. She also has to her name an essay collection, *Unauthorized Voices* (Yale, 2010), as well as eighteen books of poems translated from French.

MUHAMMAD AL-FAQIH SALEH

In 1978, the poet Muhammad al-Faqih Saleh was imprisoned along with a number of Libyan writers on charges of forming a leftist party aimed at overthrowing the regime in Libya. All accused were sentenced to life terms. In 1986, al-Faqih Saleh's sentence was changed to capital punishment, but the execution was not carried out. He and the others accused were released in March 1988 as part of a general amnesty. After being released from prison, al-Faqih Saleh was allowed to return to his post at the Libyan Ministry of Foreign Affairs. After the rebellion that toppled Muammad Qaddafi, he served as Libya's ambassador to Spain from 2012 until his death in 2017.

N. VENUGOPAL

N. Venugopal is an economist by training and a poet, literary critic, translator, journalist, columnist and public speaker by choice. In 2005, he left mainstream journalism after twenty years, to launch an alternative monthly journal of society and political economy. He has twenty-five books in Telugu and twenty-five translations from English to Telugu to his credit.

NATASHA NARWAL

Natasha Narwal is a feminist activist based in Delhi, India. She is currently pursuing a PhD at the Centre For Historical Studies, JNU. Her research looks at gendered pedagogy, space and gender. She has completed her graduation and master's in history from Hindu College, Delhi University. Narwal has been involved in various students' movements and protests in Delhi since 2006. She is a member of women students' collective Pinjra Tod and has been part of its various campaigns. She participated in the anti-CAA protests in Delhi along with thousands of women struggling for and demanding a just nation and equal citizenship for all. She was subsequently arrested in 'conspiracy' cases regarding the Delhi riots and charged under the Unlawful Activities (Prevention) Act and various other sections of the IPC. She spent almost thirteen months in Tihar Jail.

NILANJANA S. ROY

Nilanjana S. Roy is a novelist (*The Wildings*, *The Hundred Names of Darkness*), essayist ('The Girl Who Ate Books'), editor (*Our Freedoms*, *Patriots, Poets and Prisoners*, *The Penguin Book of Indian Food Writing*) and a columnist for the *Financial Times*. Her next novel, *Black River*, is out in early 2022. She lives in New Delhi.

SALIL TRIPATHI

Salil Tripathi was born in Bombay and lives in New York. He was chair of PEN International's Writers in Prison Committee (2015-2021) and is now a member of its international board. He has also been co-chair of English PEN's Writers at Risk Committee, when he lived in London. His books include *Offence: The Hindu Case*, *The Colonel Who Would Not Repent: The Bangladesh War and its Unquiet Legacy*, and *Detours: Songs of the Open Road*. He is writing a book about Gujaratis. In 2015, he received the Red Ink Award for human rights journalism from the Mumbai Press Club. In 2011, he won the third prize at the Bastiat Awards in New York. In 1994, he won an award at the Citibank Pan Asia Economic Journalism Awards. He has been a correspondent in India, Singapore and Hong Kong and has been published widely in newspapers and magazines around the world. His essays and poems have appeared in several anthologies, and he has contributed papers to academic works on human rights. Salil studied at the New Era School in Bombay and graduated from Sydenham College at the University of Bombay, and later, from the Amos Tuck School of Business Administration at Dartmouth College in the US.

SARA HOSSAIN

Sara Hossain is a barrister practicing in the Supreme Court of Bangladesh, and serves pro bono as the honorary executive director of the Bangladesh Legal Aid and Services Trust. She is a member of the Board of the United Nations Voluntary Fund for Victims of Torture, and is associated with several international civil society initiatives. Hossain writes and speaks on public interest law, human rights and women's rights and access to justice. Her articles have been published in several books and journals. She has received awards from the Lawyers Committee for Human Rights (now Human Rights First), the US State Department (Women of Courage), and has been selected as a World Economic Forum Fellow and an Asia 21 Fellow.

SARA WHYATT

Sara Whyatt is a campaigner and researcher on freedom of artistic expression and human rights. She headed PEN International's freedom of expression programme for over twenty years, during which time she campaigned for thousands of writers worldwide who had been imprisoned, attacked and even killed. She is now working on projects exploring the ways that artistic freedom is curtailed across the world, providing her expertise to a wide variety of organisations, including UNESCO, the Council of Europe and Swedish Arts Council, as well as smaller arts and human rights organisations working to support threatened artists.

SAW WAI

Saw Wai was born in 1960, and is a Buddhist. His first short story was printed in the magazine *Sar Pay Lote Thar* in 1984. He has published three collective works of poetry and one satire. In 1996, He received the Readers' Choice Award in 1996 for his poetry, published in the magazine *Ma Har Thi*, and in 2000, for his poetry in the magazine *Cherry*. In 2008, he received the PEN Award from the World Association of Writers and in 2009, was finalised for the Freedom to Create Art Award. Under military rule in Myanmar, almost a hundred of his poems were censored, and in 2008, he was imprisoned for over two years for his poem criticising the military chief commander. Saw Wai participates in installation art and performance art shows in Myanmar and ASEAN countries. He is a member of PEN Myanmar.

SHILPA GUPTA

Shilpa Gupta was born and lives in Bombay. She studied at the Sir J.J. School of Fine Art in the 1990s. Through her research-based practice, she has engaged with art in its participatory, interactive and public dimensions for over two decades. She incorporates a range of diverse material, such as text, drawings, objects, sound and interactive video to probe the ideas of borderlines, labels, censorship and security. Gupta has had solo shows at the Barbican in London, Contemporary Arts Center in Cincinnati, OK Center for Contemporary Art in Linz and Lalit Kala in New Delhi. In 2021, she had a major survey show at the Museum of Contemporary Art in Antwerp. Her work has been shown at biennales in Venice, Kochi, Berlin, Sharjah and Gwanju and at the Museum of Modern Art, Guggenheim Museum, Tate Modern, Centre Pompidou, Kiran Nadar Museum of Art amongst others. Gupta has co-curated 'Crossovers & Rewrites: Borders over Asia' at World Social Forum, Porto Alegre in 2005 and 'Aar Paar', a public art exchange project between India and Pakistan from 2002–2006. In 2004, she received the Sanskriti Prathisthan in New Delhi and International Artist of the Year, South Asian Visual Artists Collective, in Toronto; in 2018, she received the India Today New Media Artist of the Year and GQ 2019 Cultural Provocateur Award in 2019.

STELLA NYANZI

Stella Nyanzi is a multiple award-winning medical anthropologist with specialisation in sexual and reproductive health, sexual rights and human sexualities in Uganda and the Gambia. She is a radical queer feminist scholar, social justice activist, human rights defender, non-violent protester, poet, social media activist, Ugandan opposition politician belonging to the Forum for Democratic Change (FDC), a former aspirant for the seat of member of Parliament, Kampala, and mother of three teenagers. Her first poetry anthology, *No Roses From My Mouth: Poems From Prison*, was written while she was imprisoned in Uganda. She was acquitted after fifteen months.

TINA MARIE MONELYON

Tina Marie Monelyon researches and lectures on entrepreneurship and innovation at Vienna University of Economics and Business while pursuing her PhD. Driven by curiosity and her diverse interests, she has worked on projects ranging from adapting global marketing strategy to local market needs in China and India with multinational corporations, to furthering open education in Europe and art-related projects, such as the 'For, In Your Tongue, I Cannot Fit' sound installation and a workshop for children at Kochi-Muziris Biennale 2018. Tina holds an MSc in management (University of Mannheim) and has completed PG diplomas in modern and contemporary art history (Dr. Bhau Daji Lad Mumbai City Museum) and critical theory, aesthetics and practice (Jnanapravaha, Mumbai).

UMAR KHALID

Umar Khalid was born in 1987 and is an Indian activist who led the Democratic Students' Union at JNU, New Delhi. On 9 February 2016, Khalid along with other JNU students, had organised a 'poetry reading' session titled 'The country without a post office', named after Agha Shahid Ali's famous poem, to mark the third anniversary of the execution of 2001 Parliament attack convict Afzal Guru. Khalid faced sedition charges for allegedly raising anti-national slogans. He later became part of United Against Hate (UAH), a campaign that began in 2017 opposing the many acts of lynching. His academic work includes research on indigenous communities and their resistance. In 2018, he narrowly escaped an assassination attempt. On 14 September 2020, the Delhi police arrested Khalid under the UAPA, which has been used against activists, student leaders and journalists, including some writers featured in this book.

VALZHYNA MORT

Valzhyna Mort is a poet and translator born in Minsk, Belarus. Her third poetry collection, *Music for the Dead and Resurrected* (2020), received the International Griffin Poetry Prize. She is the author of Factory of *Tears and Collected Body* (Copper Canyon Press, 2008 and 2011, respectively). Mort's work has been honoured with the Lannan Fellowship, the American Academy in Rome Fellowship, and a National Endowment for the Arts translation grant. She teaches at Cornell University and writes in English and Belarusian.

VARAVARA RAO

Varavara Rao was born in 1940 and is a poet, teacher, columnist, literary critic, translator and public speaker. In his sixty-year career as a poet and write, he has published sixteen volumes of poetry and about twenty volumes of prose, including literary criticism, socio-political analysis, memoirs and translation. Between 1973 and 2018, he was implicated in twenty-five cases but the prosecution could not prove a single charge in any case and the courts acquitted or discharged him from all the cases. He had been imprisoned since August 2018 as an undertrial in the Bhima Koregaon case and was granted interim bail in August 2022.

YASSER KHANJER

Yasser Khanjer was born in 1977 in the village of Majdal Shams in the occupied Golan Heights. He was imprisoned from 1997 till 2005 by the Israeli occupation forces, on charges of resisting the occupation. His first collection of poems, *Freedom Bird*, was published in Beirut during his incarceration. Two others followed, and a fourth, *It Is Not Midway*, was published in Milan in 2017. His poems have been translated into French, English, Hebrew and German.

YUSUF ERADAM

One of the seven founders of American Studies Association of Turkey, Yusuf Eradam is a poet, essayist, awarded short-story writer, translator, photographer, theatre critic, editor and songwriter. Professor of English and American literatures for forty-four years now, Eradam has written twenty-three books, of which nine are translations, including translations of Sylvia Plath and Paul Aster. He received his BA, MA and PhD degrees from Hacettepe University, Ankara, University of Edinburgh and Moray House College of Education, Scotland, respectively. Eradam has worked at universities in Ankara, Istanbul and in the USA, and has founded and chaired departments of English, American culture and literature, and also translation studies. He lives in Istanbul with two cats: Sharab and Raki.

Credits

A sincere thanks to the many poets and their families, translators and publishers who have so generously allowed us to include poems in 'For, In Your Tongue, I Cannot Fit':

The Unavoidable Voice by Angel Cuadra, translated by Luis Ignacio Larcada. Edited by Sarah Hesketh and Cat Lucas, courtesy of the translator Luis Larcada.

A Boy Is Worth More Than A Girl by Abu Nuwas, Le Vin, le Vent, la Vie, (translated by Vincent Mansour Monteil), Paris: Sindbad, 1979, p. 91

My Mother by Nguyễn Chí Thiện, translated by Nguyen Ngoc Bich.

The Beggars' Song by Jean Richepin.

Making Our Clowns Martyrs by Jack Mapanje, *Malawi Writing Today - A PEN Anthology of Recent Writing in Malawi*, edited by Kingston Lapukeni, 1999, courtesy of the publisher PEN Malawi.

Both Worlds Can Fit Within Me by Imadeddin Nesimi.

Resist, My People, Resist Them by Dareen Tatour, translated by Terrie Dawood, courtesy of the poet.

Massacre by Liao Yiwu, translated by Michael M. Day, courtesy of Wenguang Huang, translator of *For a Song and a Hundred Songs*, and the poet.

Somehow We Survive by Dennis Brutus, courtesy of Justina Brutus Baker Robertson.

Hail, O Motherland, May Victory Always Be Yours by Ram Prasad Bismil, translated by Gopika Jadeja.

Constitution by Habib Jalib, translated by Gopika Jadeja.

Remembering a Battered Buddha by Tsering Woeser, courtesy of the translator Andrew E. Clark, © 2008 Ragged Banner Press and the poet.

Son Of Man by by Auguste-Marseille Barthélémy, courtesy of the translator Jack Cox.

Dance Your Anger And Your Joys by Ken Saro-Wiwa, courtesy of the Ken-Saro-Wiwa Foundation.

To Defy Shattering I Petrified Like A Rock by Mehdi Mousavi, courtesy of the translator Amir Khadem and the poet.

Sing Tar, Sing by Mushfig, translated by Olga Moisseyenko, *Azerbaijanian Poetry: Classic, Modern, Traditional*, edited by Mirza Ibrahimov, originally published by Progress Publishers, Moscow, www.progresspublishers.org.

Waterfall, Why Are You Lamenting by Zeb-un-Nissa, courtesy of Adil Jussawalla.

Experiencing Death by Liu Xiaobo, translated by Jeffrey Yang, from *June Fourth Elegies*, © 2012, reprinted with permission of Graywolf Press.

Time by Adonis, courtesy of the translator Kamal Abu-Deeb.

The Fray Of Stockport by Samuel Bamford, https://www.poemhunter.com/poem/the-fray-of-stockport/ (last accessed on 10 January 2022).

The Crypt by Dia'a al-Abdullah, courtesy of the translator Ghias Aljundi.

I Want to Stay Calm by Anna Barkova, courtesy of the translator Katharine Hodgson.

Our Bread by Sedigeh Vasmaghi, courtesy of the translator Milena Rampoldi, ProMosaik e.V .

Who Be Kind To by Allen Ginsberg, © 1965, Allen Ginsberg, used with permission of the Wylie Agency (UK) Limited.

Civilian And Soldier by Wole Soyinka, courtesy of the poet.

Slave of the Commonwealth, Nehru by Majrooh Sultanpuri, translated by Gopika Jadeja.

Five Bandits by Kim Chi-ha, courtesy of the translator Brother Anthony, first published in *The Colors of Dawn*, published as a special issue of *Manoa* by the University of Hawaií Press, 2016.

Glory To Those Who Torture Us by Abdellatif Laâbi, translated by André Naffis-Sahely, © 2018, André Naffis-Sahely, courtesy of the Wylie Agency (UK) Limited and the poet.

Brother Negro by Regino Pedroso, courtesy of the translator John A. Gronbeck-Tedesco.

A letter to 1921: for Nikolai Gumilev by Irina Ratushinskaya, courtesy of the translator Ian Probstein and the estate of Irina Ratushinskaya.

On the Infinite, the Universe, and the Worlds: Five Cosmological Dialogues by Giordano Bruno, published by Huginn, Munnin & Co., Ohio, 2014, courtesy the translator Scott Gosnell.

Love's Web by Rabi'a Balkhi, courtesy of the translator Bashir Sakhwaraz.

February 14 by Saw Wai, translated and published by *Harper's Magazine* (USA), March 2010, courtesy of the poet.

Che Guevara by Metin Demirtaş, courtesy of the translator Yusuf Eradam.

Stark Electric Jesus by Malay Roychoudhury, translation courtesy of the poet.

And So Your Poetry Must by Ericson Acosta, courtesy of Emmanuel Acosta.

Bad News On A Scrap Of Newspaper by Roque Dalton, courtesy of the translator Kelly Washbourne.

The Killing Of The She-Camel by Hadraawi, translated for the Poetry Translation Centre by W.N. Herbert, Said Jamal Hussein and Maxamed Xasan 'Alto', courtesy of the Poetry Translation Centre.

Coming Of Anondomoyee by Kazi Nazrul Islam, published in *Kazi Nazrul Islam: Selected Works*, Nazrul Institute, Dhaka: Bangladesh, 1999, courtesy of the translator Sajed Kamal.

The Soldier And The Snow by Miguel Hernández Gilabert, from *The Selected Poems Of Miguel Hernandez*, translated By Timothy Baland, White Pine Press, 1995, courtesy of the publisher.

Image by Maung Saung Kha, courtesy of the translator Ko Ko Thett and the poet.

Jasmine Revolution Poem by Mohammad al-Ajami Ibn al-Dhib, courtesy of the translator Kareem James Abu-Zeid.

Run by Fatemeh Ekhtesari, courtesy the translator Mohammad Hosseini Moghaddam and the poet.

The Brave Hedgehog by Daniil Kharms, *Russian Absurd: The Selected Writings of Daniil Kharms*, Northwestern University Press, 2017, courtesy of the translator Alex Cigale.

The Last of the Line of Refugee Descendants by Ashraf Fayadh, translated by Jonathan Wright, The Operating System, courtesy of the publisher.

Singing Solo by Huang Xiang, courtesy of translator Michelle Yeh.

Stalin's Epigram by Osip Mandelstam, courtesy of the translator by Ian Probstein.

Identity Card by Mahmoud Darwish, translated by Salman Hilmy, courtesy Washington Report on Middle East Affairs.

Tomorrow Maybe They Will Kill Us by Yannis Ritsos, adaption by Nikos Xilouris.

The Scourge of War by Amanuel Asrat, translated by Tedros Abraham in collaboration with David Shook, courtesy of the translators.

A Banner For The Revolution by Martin Carter, *University Of Hunger: Collected Poems And Selected Prose*, edited by Gemma Robinson Bloodaxe Books, 2006, courtesy of the publisher.

City of No Voice by Nâzim Hikmet, courtesy of the translator Yusuf Eradam and the poet's family.

A Sonnet Written for One Who Died by the Holy Office in Rome by Tommaso Campanella, courtesy of the translator Sherry Roush, professor of italian, Penn State University, University Park.

Khalifa by Ayat al-Qurmezi, translated by Ghias Aljundi with Mitchell Albert, https://pen.org/give-us-back-our-bahrain-2/ (last accessed on 10 January 2021).

Wishes by Ajmal Khattak, courtesy of the translator Najib Manalai.

The Tennis Player in the Moment by César Vallejo, courtesy of the translator Dave Bonta.

Speak by Faiz Ahmad Faiz, translated by Victor G. Kiernan, courtesy of Heather Kiernan. Special thanks to Faiz Foundation Trust Pakistan.

A sincere thanks to those who have so generously allowed us to include the following pieces, first published by them, in 'For, In Your Tongue, I Cannot Fit':

Poetry by Varavara Rao, translated from Telugu by N. Venugopal, published in *Muktakantham*, Samudram Prachuranalu, Vijayawada, 1990.

It Would Not Have Been by Muhammad al-Faqih Saleh, translated from Arabic by Khaled Mattawa, published in *Qasa'id Al-Zhul* (Shadow Poems), 2016.

'Prison Diary: Uncertainty Keeps Political Prisoners Hanging Between Hope and Hopelessness' by Umar Khalid, first published in *Outlook*, 11 January 2022.

Every possible effort has been made to identify and reach out to the respective copyright holders. In case you have any query regarding this, we welcome you to contact us.

Book credits

Published by: Westland Books
Edited by: Shilpa Gupta and Salil Tripathi
Design: Shilpa Gupta and Saurabh Garge
Editorial assistance: Czetan Patil,
Pooja Tilve and Pranav Gogwekar
Coordination support:
Tina Marie Monelyon

Photographer credits

Pat Verbruggen: pp. xiv–xvi, xxxvi, 1, 41, 61, 301
Czetan Patil: pp. 16, 21, 49, 62–67, 242-247, 271
Johnny Barrington: p. v
Max Colson: pp. 283, 293
Siddhant Pitale: p. 257

List of artworks

'For, In Your Tongue, I Cannot Fit', 2017–18
Sound installation with 100 speakers, microphones, printed text and metal stands.
1500 x 1500 x 400 cm | 600 x 600 x 150 in
Co-commissioned by YARAT Contemporary Art Space and Edinburgh Art Festival with support from QAGOMA
pp. v, xiv-xvi,1,61

Untitled, 2021
Polymer resin
18 x 10.5 x 5 cm | 7 x 4 x 2 in
p. 16

Untitled, 2018
A spoken poem in a bottle, photograph
152.5 x 18 x 30.5 cm | 60 x 7 x 12 in
p. 41

Untitled, 2020—2021
Gun metal
24 x 28 x 10 cm | 9.5 x 11 x 4 in
p. 271

Untitled (Distance Between Two Tears), 2021
Aluminum, steel
6.8 x 2.5 x 0.38 cm | 2.7 x 1 x 0.15 in
p. 49

Visitor Hours, 2020–2021
Gun metal
20 x 0.5 x 7 cm | 7.8 x 0.19 x 2.7 in
p. 271

Untitled, 2021
Interlocked books (without glue)
23 x 23 x 149 cm | 9 x 9 x 58 in
p. 293

A Liquid, the Mouth Froze, 2018
Cast of open mouth in gun metal, etched brass plate
17.5 x 11 x 18.5 cm | 6.9 × 4.3 × 7.3 in
p. 21

Untitled (Tower of Broken Pencil Points), 2021
Pencil leads
18 x 18 x 137 cm | 7 x 7 x 54 in
p. 283

Words Come From Ears, 2018
Motion Flapboard
17x96x5 in | 43x244x13 cm, 15 mins loop
p.301

Untitled
Tracings on paper, 2018–ongoing
31 x 22 x 3 cm | 12 × 8.6 × 1.18 in each